EXPLOR
THE KENNET AND AVON
CANAL

Nigel Vile

COUNTRYSIDE BOOKS
NEWBURY, BERKSHIRE

Countryside Books' walking guides cover most areas of England and Wales and include the following series:

County Rambles
Walks For Motorists
Exploring Long Distance Paths
Literary Walks

A complete list is available from the publishers.

Also by Nigel Vile

Avon Rambles
Gloucestershire Rambles
Somerset Rambles

First Published 1991
© Nigel Vile 1991
Reprinted and updated 1992

COUNTRYSIDE BOOKS
3 Catherine Road
Newbury, Berkshire

ISBN 1 85306 124 7

Cover photograph of Bathampton
taken by Martin Brown
Sketch maps by the author

Produced through MRM Associates Ltd., Reading
Printed by JW Arrowsmith Ltd., Bristol

Contents

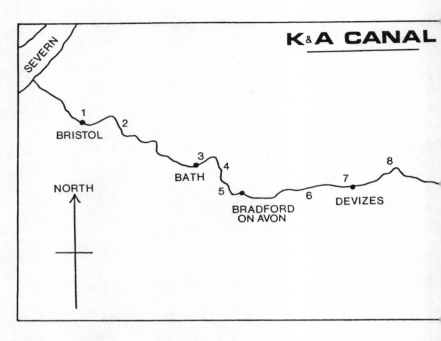

K&A CANAL

SEVERN

1 BRISTOL 2

3 BATH 4

5 6 BRADFORD ON AVON

7 DEVIZES 8

NORTH

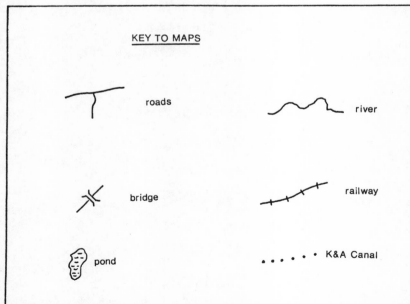

KEY TO MAPS

roads

river

bridge

railway

pond

K&A Canal

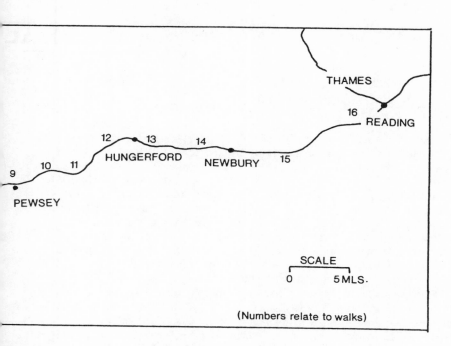

THAMES

16   READING

12   13   14
HUNGERFORD   NEWBURY   15

9   10   11

PEWSEY

SCALE

0   5 MLS.

(Numbers relate to walks)

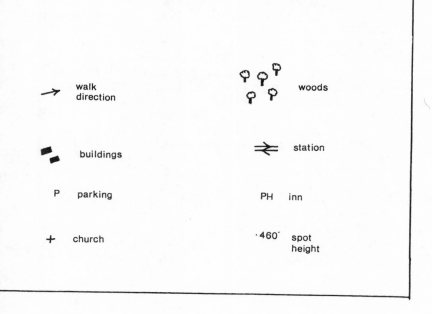

→   walk
      direction

woods

buildings

⇌   station

P   parking

PH   inn

+   church

·460·   spot
        height

Introduction

When canal mania gripped Britain in the late 18th century, it did not go unnoticed even in the normally sedate West Country. A simple advertisement in a Salisbury journal in 1792, announcing a meeting in Devizes to discuss a proposed waterway to Bristol, caused businessmen from that city to head into the depths of the Wiltshire countryside. An infamous 'Ride to Devizes' ensued, that was immortalised by at least two local poets of the time! There was clearly no shortage of venture capital, attracted by the high returns that investors had earned on such investments elsewhere in Britain. A line was surveyed by the engineer John Rennie, Royal Assent was granted in 1794, and in the same year work began on the Kennet and Avon Canal.

The river Kennet between Newbury and Reading had been navigable since the early 18th century, as had the Avon Navigation between Bath and Bristol. All that remained was to bridge the gap between Bath and Newbury, a mere 57 miles, and London would have a direct link with Bristol. With the exception of the 16 locks that make up the Caen Hill flight at Devizes, the K & A was completed by 1807. Temporarily, a tramway lifted the barges up this famous incline. By 1810, work on Caen Hill was completed and the *Bath Herald* was able to report that 'the guns were fired on Sydney Wharf' alongside the canal's headquarters in Cleveland House.

Traffic on the canal followed an all too familiar pattern. There was an initial boom – the canal carried 341,878 tons of freight in 1838, for example. The main cargo was coal, moved to the K & A by means of the Somerset Coal Canal from Radstock and Paulton. There followed inevitable competition from the railways, with the Great Western Railway opening its line between London and Bristol in 1841. Canal tolls were slashed and redundancies were declared, the losses mounted up and eventually the K & A was sold to the GWR for a princely £210,415! The canal was deliberately run down and neglected so that by 1955 the Rusholme survey listed it as grade III – 'canals which are either disused or carry insufficient trade to justify their retention as commercial waterways.'

In the post-war years, the Kennet and Avon Canal Trust has worked closely with the British Waterways Board to breathe fresh life into this great waterway. Lock gates have been replaced, lock chambers re-bricked, leaking canal beds lined with concrete and any number of YTS trainees have been equipped with basic manual skills while undertaking restoration work. All of this sweat and toil was rewarded in August 1990 when the Queen journeyed west to Devizes to officially re-open the K & A Canal. Forty years of dedication and hard work have produced a national asset that will undoubtedly attract thousands of visitors to the canal, a veritable jewel in the BWB's vast network of inland waterways.

Just what can the visitor to the K & A expect to find? Between Bath and Bradford-on-Avon, the canal passes through the magnificent Avon Valley where steeply wooded hillsides tumble down to the river bank. This same section of canal can boast two of the finest aqueducts on Britain's canal network, at Dundas and Avoncliff, both carrying the K & A across the Bristol Avon. Dundas is also the junction with the Somerset Coal Canal, whose first 400 yards have been lovingly restored to provide moorings for the many pleasure craft that cruise the waterway at an unhurried four miles per hour.

Further east at Caen Hill, just on the edge of Devizes, lies the remarkable flight of 16 locks formed like an actual staircase. Such was the pressure that these locks placed on the water supply that each lock was built with a side pound to act as a reservoir. These pounds today provide a haven for wildlife, including the majestic heron. The Caen Hill flight was so busy with commercial traffic that gaslights were installed to enable the locks to be used 24 hours a day – provided the bargees could afford the extra shilling that was charged after dark!

The summit of the canal is at Crofton, just south of Marlborough, where a local stretch of water, Wilton Water, was tapped as a reservoir. Wilton Water lay 40 ft beneath the canal's summit, which meant that a pumping station was needed. A pair of Boulton and Watt beam pumping engines were installed that were capable of raising one ton of water with every stroke, each engine running at 12 strokes a minute. During summer weekends and on bank-holidays, these engines are still in steam, the oldest working steam engines in the world.

For walkers, the canal not only offers an insight into Britain's vast industrial heritage, it also passes through fine walking country. In addition to the Avon Valley, the K & A also passes through the rich and fertile Vale of Pewsey, overlooked by the imposing North Wessex Downs. Further east, the canal touches the southern fringes of Savernake Forest, before making for Great Bedwyn, Hungerford and the Berkshire downlands.

This book offers the rambler 16 circular walks along the length of the K & A between Bristol and Reading. The circuits have been selected not necessarily to provide the most scenic landscapes, but rather to offer as varied a selection of canalside environments as possible. This explains why, for example, Walk 2 passes through an urban part of Bristol, whilst further east several tranquil rural rounds were neglected. Being a bargee was not just a working holiday! Each circuit offers a towpath section as well as an exploration of the local towns or villages or countryside that would have been influenced by the canal. This means that the guide will be as useful to the water-borne traveller wishing to explore a little of the countryside through which he is passing, as to the rambler. The walks are arranged in a logical west to east order, starting in the City Docks in Bristol and culminating at Kennet Mouth in Reading. Each towpath section is similarly followed in an easterly direction to give a feeling of continuity and direction.

Each of the 16 rambles comes complete with details of parking and refreshment arrangements, together with estimates of the distance to be covered. Access by public transport is possible as several of the walks start near railway stations but availability of trains would have to be checked with British Rail, especially at weekends. The timing for a ramble will, of course, depend upon the nature of the individual or group concerned. Two miles in an hour is a leisurely pace, 3½ miles an hour and the old brow would be perspiring quite quickly! A personal selection of historical notes has been included to enable the landscapes and landmarks, the villages and the people to be placed into some sort of historical context. Each ramble was planned using the Ordnance Survey 1:25 000 Pathfinder series of maps, that show clearly the public rights-of-way. For those walkers who like to carry either this series of maps, or the 1:50 000 Landranger sheets, with them, each walk also contains details of the relevant sheets.

I was born just five miles from the City Docks in Bristol, at the western end of the waterway, and much of my life has been spent in the proximity of the K & A. As a schoolboy, I spent many an hour clearing out rubbish and debris from the derelict canal bed on the outskirts of Bath. I am currently living at Bradford-on-Avon, just half a mile from the towpath, and work in the City of Bath where the K & A joins the river Avon. Over the past few years I have witnessed what had become a muddy ditch being transformed into a living and vibrant waterway. It has been a magnificent achievement, and one which I hope that you will enjoy as you follow the circuits outlined in this volume. May I wish you many happy and relaxing hours of walking.

Nigel A Vile
March 1991

Bristol Floating Harbour – Key

1 – Arnolfini Arts Centre
2 – Industrial Museum
3 – Maritime Heritage Centre and SS *Great Britain*
4 – Bathurst Basin
5 – St Mary Redcliffe Church
6 – St Nicholas' Church Museum
7 – The Corn Exchange
8 – Hippodrome Theatre
9 – The Council House and College Green
10 – Bristol Cathedral and the Central Library

START

Bristol Bridge

Welsh Back

Anchor Road

Canon's Marsh

Floating Harbour

Cumberland Road

River Avon

New Cut

N

Scale

0   ¼ mile

The Floating Harbour, Bristol

Introduction: Bristol's wealth and prosperity can be traced historically to her great seafaring tradition. The slave trade, a shameful
chapter in the city's history, forged links with the West Indies and the
Americas. Out of these links grew many of the city's historic industries – tobacco, sugar, chocolate and sherry being but the best known
examples. This seafaring tradition was brought right to the heart of
the city by way of the navigable river Avon. Although the old City
Docks can no longer accommodate today's vast sea-going vessels, the
old quays and wharves in the city centre still convey the atmosphere
of an historic seaport. This walk explores the city's Floating Harbour,
now a vast leisure amenity, as well as venturing away from the water's
edge to discover some of Bristol's attractions that include St Mary
Redcliffe church and the Anglican cathedral. This is an urban landscape, where traffic and noise are ever present, but these intrusions
represent but a small price to pay for the privilege of exploring one of
England's great city centres.

Distance: A short circuit of little over 3 miles. However, visitors who
fully explore all of the sites on the route could well fill a whole day.
Maps: OS Landranger 172 'Bristol & Bath'; OS Pathfinder ST 47/57
'Portishead & Bristol West'.

Refreshments: You will not walk for more than 10 minutes on this
route without passing a pub, cafe or restaurant. It is even possible to
satisfy your appetite on board a floating hostelry!

How to get there: The walk begins at Canon's Marsh, a vast carpark
just off the city centre behind the cathedral. Parking is not cheap,
except on Sundays when no fee is charged. (GR 583 725)

WALK ONE

The Walk: From Canon's Marsh carpark, aim for the quayside that lies to the immediate left-hand side of the new Lloyds Bank building. This will bring you onto St Augustine's Reach alongside the Lochiel Floating Restaurant. Turn left and follow the quayside around to the Arnolfini Arts Centre on the opposite side of the Reach, walking initially along the western side of the waterway where the converted warehouses now function as shops, cafes, and much else besides.

Cross the water where it enters a tunnel to meander beneath the city centre, and turn right to walk along the eastern side of St Augustine's Reach, past the Unicorn Hotel, to the Arnolfini. Cross the Floating Harbour by means of Princes Street Bridge, alongside the Arts Centre, and turn right to follow the quayside in front of the Industrial Museum. Continue along the water's edge for several hundred yards until you reach the Maritime Heritage Centre and the SS *Great Britain*.

Just past the Heritage Centre, turn left and follow Gas Ferry Road to its junction with Cumberland Road. Turn right and join the footpath that runs alongside the New Cut by means of the footbridge a short distance ahead. Follow the New Cut upstream (i.e. walk back on yourself), initially using the footpath that later joins the roadside pavement. The New Cut is an artificial channel dug to carry the Avon's tidal waters whilst the Floating Harbour is sealed off using lock gates. You will soon reach Bathurst Bridge, spanning a one-time link between the Cut and the Harbour. Cross the road to Bathurst Basin, and follow its quayside past the General Hospital and the Ostrich Inn to a flight of steps on the right-hand side.

At the top of the steps, continue along Redcliffe Parade to Redcliffe Hill and St Mary Redcliffe church. Fortunately, there is a pedestrian crossing for the brief detour across the main road to what Queen Elizabeth I described as 'England's finest Parish Church'. Turn left on reaching Redcliffe Hill, left again at the roundabout, and cross the Floating Harbour using Redcliffe Bridge. Immediately, turn right into a turning called Welsh Back, a name that is derived from the local coastal trade in centuries past. At the first opportunity, turn right through a gap in the offices alongside Welsh Back to reach the quayside. Follow the waterside path until it reaches Baldwin Street and St Nicholas' Church Museum.

Climb the steps to the left of the church, and continue along All Saints Lane and through the covered market area to Corn Street. Turn left and follow Corn Street to the city centre. Cross to the Hippodrome Theatre using the street crossings. Pass in front of the

12

Hippodrome and take the first turning on the right into Denmark Street. Harveys Bristol Cream, sherry importers, still have their headquarters in this narrow side street, a reminder of the traditional port-based industries. Turn left at Unity Street, and you will shortly reach the foot of Park Street.

Cross over this main thoroughfare to College Green, walk in front of the Council House and continue towards the cathedral. Between the cathedral and the Central Library, an archway leads into College Square. Follow the road from this point down to Anchor Road, where directly opposite you will find Canon's Marsh carpark.

Historical Notes

Bristol: The Anglo-Saxons named their settlement 'Bricgstow', literally 'the settlement by the bridge'. The advantages of the site were clear – a well-drained mound, 6 miles inland where shipping could find a safe anchorage. It was this ability to serve as a port that was to account for the city's growth and prosperity.

By the 15th century, Bristol was exporting large quantities of cloth, all of which was produced in the city's hinterland by the local West of England woollen industry. Trade with countries such as France, Spain and Portugal led to wine becoming a major import. The city's wealthy merchants at that time financed the construction of some of Bristol's great buildings, St Mary Redcliffe church being but the best known case in point.

The development of a fish trade with Iceland meant that legends of uncharted lands to the west began to reach what was at the time England's leading provincial port. The city's merchants were soon promoting exploratory voyages across the Atlantic, and it was not long before explorers such as John Cabot were returning with stories of the New World – literally a 'new-found-land'.

Bristol was heavily involved in the 17th century slave trade. Vessels from the city shipped Negroes from the African west coast across to the West Indies. In return for selling fellow members of the human race into a life of captivity and bondage, the ships would return to the West Country laden with cargoes of rum, sugar and tobacco. It was an evil trade that was to make Bristol the wealthiest provincial city.

Towards the end of the 18th century, however, the city's fortunes were to take a turn for the worse. Trade with the Americas diminished due to the war with America that took place between 1775 and

13

1781, whilst 1833 saw the abolition of the Slave Trade. This was also the era of the Industrial Revolution, which largely bypassed the West of England. Liverpool, the largest port in the north, was making great inroads into Bristol's traditional trade. The Mersey port was largely unaffected by the sort of tides that handicapped navigation on the river Avon.

Attempts were made to revive Bristol's flagging fortunes. Lock gates were installed at either end of what became known as the 'Floating Harbour', and a 'New Cut' was dug to carry the tidal waters of the Avon to the south of the port. Unfortunately, the privately owned Dock Company responsible for these improvements found that the cost of constructing the New Cut and forming the Floating Harbour came to double the original estimates. The subsequent harbour dues were so high that trade dwindled still further! A somewhat ironic example of this was provided by Brunel's Great Western Steamship Company. The *Great Western*, a Bristol-built paddle steamer, was originally constructed to link up with the Great Western Railway to provide a direct link with New York. The level of charges at the Port of Bristol were so high that the *Great Western* actually ended up operating out of Liverpool!

With the growth in the size of vessels, the tortuous journey down the Avon to the City Docks became ever more unpopular. The construction of new port facilities at the mouth of the river, at Avonmouth and Portishead, became inevitable. From the turn of the 20th century, the dock's future was becoming ever more precarious.

Today, all commercial shipping is handled by Avonmouth and Royal Portbury Docks. The Floating Harbour has become a vast leisure amenity in the heart of the city. Many of its attractions are included on this walk – the SS *Great Britain*, the Bristol Harbour Railway, the Maritime Heritage Centre, Bathurst Basin and the Industrial Museum. So rich and varied are the attractions, visitors are well advised to invest in a copy of the city's *Official Visitors' Guide*.

The section of the walk between Welsh Back and Canon's Marsh explores some of the historic streets around the old docks. Once again, the list of attractions is so large that purchasing the official guidebook to the city is the wisest course of action. Amongst the many landmarks are St Nicholas' Church Museum, St Nicholas' Market, the Corn Exchange, the City Centre, College Green and the Cathedral. On most other walks, just one of these attractions would constitute a feature of note!

The River Avon –
Bristol to Keynsham

Introduction: From the City Docks in Bristol, the river Avon heads off in a south-easterly direction towards Bath and the Kennet and Avon Canal. This linear walk follows the navigable Avon from Temple Meads Station in the heart of Bristol upstream as far as Keynsham, a town forever immortalised by Horace Batchelor's advertisements on Radio Luxembourg in the 1960s! The first couple of miles of the route passes through busy streets, bustling industrial zones and an all too typical urban landscape. Beyond Netham Lock, however, the river plunges into a tight wooded valley where the proximity of one of England's great cities is soon forgotten. East of the Chequers Inn at Hanham, the valley opens up and the Avon forges a vast loop around Keynsham Hams, all the while in the shadow of the vast Cadbury Schweppes factory that generates any number of fragrant aromas! Keynsham Lock, where we bid farewell to the navigation, lies just 5 minutes walk from the local station and the end of the walk.

Distance: A linear walk of 7½ miles, that will take 2½ to 3 hours to complete. Maps: OS Landranger 172 'Bristol & Bath'; OS Pathfinder ST 47/57 'Portishead & Bristol (West)', 1167 'Bristol (East)' and ST 66/76 'Bath & Keynsham'.

Refreshments: Towards the end of the walk there are a number of hostelries to quench your thirst or satisfy your appetite. Alongside Hanham Lock are the Chequers Inn and the Old Lock and Weir, whilst just beyond Keynsham Lock is the Lock Keeper Free House.

How to get there: With parking in Central Bristol both problematic and expensive, the best way to tackle this walk is to park at Keyn-

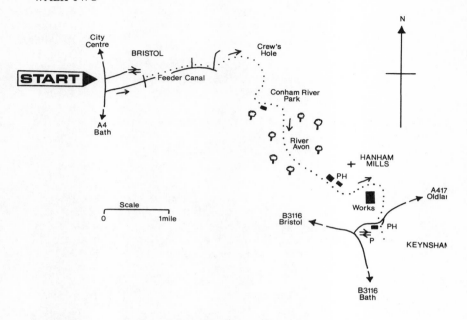

sham Station and to initially catch the train to Bristol Temple Meads. Keynsham Station lies alongside the A4175 road from the town centre to Willsbridge. There is ample free parking at the station. (GR 656 688)

The Walk: From the imposing frontage of Temple Meads Station, head down Approach Road to the busy Temple Gate. Turn left and, in a short distance, left again into Cattle Market Road. The pavement heads into a tunnel that runs underneath the railway tracks, before emerging alongside the main postal sorting office for Bristol. Continue to a busy crossroads, where traffic-lights control the traffic flow, and head straight across along Feeder Road. The Feeder Canal is on your left-hand side. In one mile, the Feeder joins the Avon beyond Netham Lock. Cross the road bridge alongside the lock and, almost immediately, turn right onto the riverside path signposted 'Avon Walkway'.

For the next 5 miles, literally follow the path alongside the north bank of the river, taking care on the short section of road walking just before Conham River Park. Beyond Conham, the path passes the site

16

of Hanham Colliery Wharf, Hanham Lock and the Chequers Inn, and the Cadbury Schweppes factory, before reaching Keynsham Lock.

The riverside path passes under the modern road bridge just beyond the lock before climbing to join the 'old' road alongside the Lock Keeper public house. Turn left along this 'old' road for a few yards, and then turn left onto the busy A4175 as it crosses the Avon before climbing into Keynsham. Just 250 yards beyond the river, the local railway station lies on the left-hand side.

Historical Notes

Temple Meads Station in Bristol was built to the designs of Sir Matthew Digby Wyatt in 1878. The station buildings accommodate a sharp bend where the Great Western Railway linked in with the Bristol & Exeter Railway. The clock tower that dominates the station building lost its high Victorian roof during bombing raids in the Second World War. Despite this destruction, however, the station frontage is still most impressive from an architectural point of view. Alongside today's working station lies the original terminus building of Brunel's Great Western Railway. It is believed to be the oldest surviving terminus in the country. In 1966, it was actually threatened with demolition. Sense prevailed, however, and it is now beautifully restored and functioning as an exhibition centre. It is quite rightly recognised as being an outstanding historic railway monument.

'Behind the highly decorative neo-Tudor facade, a cast-iron columned engine shed gives way to the train shed. The 72 ft central span of the timber roof is flanked by 20 ft aisles over the platform, all part of a cantilever construction often described as a hammerbeam roof from its superficial appearance.'

A Guide to the Industrial Heritage of Avon
Joan Day

The Feeder Canal is a 1 mile section of artificial waterway that bypasses a meandering stretch of the river Avon just to the south. The Feeder was cut as part of the improvements sanctioned by the Bristol Dock Act of 1803. As well as being an aid to navigation, this artificial cut was also developed to supply Bristol's Floating Harbour (see Walk 1) with fresh water, and hence prevent its stagnation.

17

Passing through a highly industrialised part of Bristol, however, it was seldom able to provide the fresh water that was intended! A century ago, the *Bristol Mercury* recorded the fact that the area around the Feeder was 'the chosen home of the manure manufacturers, the bone crushing mills, the knackers' yards and the horse flesh boiling factories' that caused 'stench-laden folds of air to envelope the visitor'. Beyond Netham Lock, the Feeder rejoins the Avon and the river passes through Crew's Hole. This was another 18th and 19th century industrial complex where coal mines stood cheek by jowl with tar manufacturers and other assorted purveyors of industrial wealth. Today, the area is being redeveloped with desirable riverside properties. Trooper's Hill Chimney, a prominent landmark on the hilltop, stands as a solitary reminder of the industrial past. The chimney was part of a sulphur extraction flue system leading from an 18th century copper works lurking somewhere in the depths of Crew's Hole.

Hanham Lock, opposite the Chequers and the Old Lock and Weir Inns at Hanham Mills, is officially the first lock on the Kennet and Avon Canal. A hundred yards downstream of the lock, the British Waterways Board hand over control of the waters to the Port of Bristol Authority. Such divisions, however, are simply a modern development, for historically the river between Bristol and Bath was all part of the Avon Navigation. The relevant Act of Parliament to improve navigation on the Avon was passed in 1712, and by 1727 the six locks that overcome the rise of 30 ft between Bristol and Bath were constructed. There had always been trade along the river, but this had been hindered by both droughts and the many shallows due to the river's mills. The local coal miners were displeased at the large volume of Shropshire coal that began to appear in the area courtesy of the new navigation. Having travelled to the West Country by way of the river Severn, it was seen as a clear threat to their livelihood. The miners' reactions were sometimes violent, and included on one occasion the destruction of the lock at nearby Saltford. None of the culprits were apprehended, which was probably as well with 'damaging the navigation' being an offence that carried the death penalty.

The vast red-brick **Cadbury Schweppes** factory dominates the final approach to Keynsham. The factory was originally owned by JS Fry and Sons, local chocolate manufacturers, whose origins can be traced back as far as 1731. In that year, a Mr Walter Churchman of Narrow

Wine Street in Bristol took out patents for the manufacture of chocolate. These patents later passed into the hands of a Mr Joseph Fry and the rest, as they say, is history. The firm was originally located in the centre of Bristol. The cramped site, with poor access, proved inadequate when it came to meeting the company's expansion plans. As a consequence, the factory was relocated to Keynsham in 1923, on a greenfield site alongside the main London to Bristol railway. Such 'garden factories' were in vogue in the early years of the 20th century, when altruistic employers were seeking to offer their workers previously undreamt of housing and recreational facilities.

Londonderry Wharf, opposite the Cadbury Schweppes factory, was the terminus of the Avon & Gloucestershire Railway, a horse-drawn tramway used for transporting coal from Coalpit Heath to the river Avon. It opened in 1832 and, although long abandoned, can still offer much of interest for the industrial archaeologist. Interested readers are referred to the relevant pages in CG Maggs' book on the Bristol & Gloucester Railway, published by the Oakwood Press.

Keynsham Lock bypasses Keynsham's Avon Mill weir. It retains a small accompanying road bridge, dating from about 1810, which today terminates at the Lock Keeper Inn. An original medieval bridge that spanned the main course of the river Avon was breached by serious flooding in 1968. It was subsequently replaced by today's modern road bridge, which is functional but would win no prizes for architectural merit!

Georgian Bath and The Widcombe Locks

Introduction: The city of Bath, famous for its Roman Baths and elegant Georgian architecture, marks the point at which the Kennet and Avon Canal (K & A) officially leaves the river Avon. A flight of six locks carries the K & A up and out of the city, through the secluded and shady Sydney Gardens. In order to blend in with these delightful surroundings, the canal company had to construct a pair of intricate iron footbridges across the canal, as well as ensuring that the entrances to the Sydney Gardens Tunnel were formed of ornately carved and decorated Bath stone. This short walk also includes a stroll along Pulteney Street, one of the most magnificent Georgian streets to be found in Britain, together with a riverside walk along the banks of the Avon downstream of Pulteney Bridge. This is altogether a quite superb town-trail that will leave you in no doubt as to why visitors have been flocking to this most beautiful of cities for close on 2,000 years.

Distance: An extremely short 2 mile walk along generally level paths. It is, in fact, a perfect Sunday afternoon stroll! Maps: OS Landranger 172 'Bristol & Bath'; OS Pathfinder ST 66/76 'Bath & Keynsham'.

Refreshments: With the centre of Bath just minutes away from the end of this walk, it goes without saying that there are many cafes, pubs and tea-shops in which to satisfy your appetite.

How to get there: The walk starts at Pulteney Bridge, one of Bath's best known landmarks. Two hour free parking is available in the adjoining Pulteney Street (no limit on Sundays). Two hours should prove adequate time in which to complete this circuit. (GR 752 649)

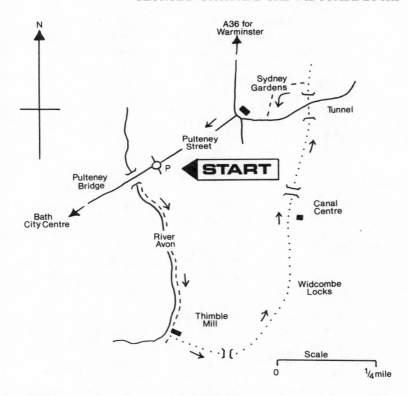

The Walk: At the eastern end of Pulteney Bridge, a flight of steps signposted to the 'Riverside Walk' brings you to the river bank alongside the Horseshoe Falls. Follow the Avon downstream for ½ mile, passing under North Parade Road and the main London to Bristol railway. Just beyond the Thimble Mill Restaurant, the K & A Canal leaves the river Avon.

Follow the canal towpath to the left for the next mile, as the K & A climbs up through the Widcombe Locks. The path changes banks on three occasions on this section of canal: at Bath Deep Lock, the path switches by means of a 'bridge' on the bottom lock gates; at Bathwick Hill, you leave the towpath temporarily, cross the main road and rejoin the opposite bank of the canal; at the entrance to the tunnel beneath Cleveland House, the towpath crosses a bridge to rejoin the western side of the canal.

21

Having passed through the tunnel and beneath the first ornate footbridge within Sydney Gardens, look for a gate on the left-hand side. Climb the steps into the gardens, cross the railway line ahead and turn immediately to the left to follow the tarmac path out of the gardens and onto Sydney Place.

Turn right, cross the busy A36 and continue straight down the road opposite – the magnificent Georgian terraces of Pulteney Street. At its far end, just beyond Laura Place and the fountain, is Pulteney Bridge where the walk began.

Historical Notes

Bath is a city whose fame has spread far beyond these shores, as is evident from the coach parties of American and Japanese tourists who flock to the city each summer. *Aquae Sulis* to the Romans, the Roman Baths were constructed around what is the only natural hot spring in Britain. It is as a spa that the city has attracted the visitor down through the years, the Regency era and its association with Beau Nash closely rivalling its fame as a Roman settlement. The city's crowning glory is its Georgian architecture, with the Royal Crescent, the Circus, Pulteney Bridge and Pulteney Street being some of the finest examples of such architecture in Britain, if not the world. Pulteney Street and Pulteney Bridge feature on this walk. Pulteney Bridge is lined with attractive shops, whose display windows overlook the Horseshoe Falls on the Avon below. The river influenced the construction of Pulteney Street, which was built over the Avon's flood-plain. A raised 'platform' was a vital ingredient in the street's construction, a precautionary device against potential flooding. It is the work of Thomas Baldwin, and represents a 'refined, lighter and more ornamental style' of the Classical Palladian form. Constructed of the golden Bath stone, the vast terraces of Pulteney Street that link Laura Place with the Holbourne of Menstrie Museum, are an unforgettable sight when bathed in the orange glow of an autumnal sunset. A book of this nature can but touch upon the grandeur of a city such as Bath. A whole library of titles exists on the city, including *Georgian Summer: the Rise and Development of Bath* by David Gadd, also published by Countryside Books.

Widcombe Locks – numbers 7 to 13 on the canal – carry the K & A from the river Avon up a not inconsiderable rise of 65 ft out of the city. Rather mysteriously, one of the locks is apparently 'missing' with Bath Lower, Bath Deep, Wash House, Abbey View, Pulteney and Bath Top making just six locks in total! The answer lies in the fact that locks 8 and 9 were combined as part of a road improvement scheme in this part of the city back in the 1970s. The resulting Bath Deep Lock, with a rise/fall of 19 ft 5 in, is the deepest canal lock in Britain. The Widcombe Locks are certainly some of the most attractive to be found on our canal network, with a pleasing blend of stone and ironwork, ornate iron bridges and delicate canalside architecture. The latter includes a fine example of a lock-keeper's cottage. Lock number 11, Abbey View, brings with it fine views across the city, whilst its side pound is a haven for wildfowl. Locks consume vast quantities of water, and a flight such as Widcombe is no exception. At the foot of the flight, alongside the junction with the Avon, lies Thimble Mill. Steam pumps once raised water from here to the top of the flight, but the only steam pouring forth from the mill now is from its kitchen – the finely restored building now functions as a restaurant! The K & A deserves all the support it can muster. With this in mind, all visitors should call in at the Canal Centre, just alongside the Top Lock. A small but comprehensive collection of canal literature is available for sale, together with friendly advice and information on the canal.

Sydney Gardens were established as a pleasure resort in 1795. A 19 acre site that contained an hotel, a bowling green and a labyrinth, this was very much an outpost of fashionable Bath. The leisured classes, partaking of Bath's genteel elegance and curative waters, would be carried in their sedan chairs to the gardens, past the elegant terraces of Pulteney Street. The prospect of a canal being cut through such an obvious beauty spot must have come as something of a shock to the city's burghers, who demanded compensation to the tune of 2,000 guineas. A pleasing blend of architectural styles were used to dampen the impact of the K & A upon the gardens, making its presence somewhat more harmonious than was feared. Two short tunnels with decorative faces, combine with a pair of ornamental footbridges to create perhaps the most magical location along the K & A's length. Above the first tunnel sits Cleveland House, built for the Duke of Cleveland in the early 19th century. This served at one time as the canal company's headquarters, with the opening in the tunnel roof allegedly acting as a trap-door through which correspondence passed from canal officials to passing bargees. The Sydney Gardens Hotel has subsequently become the Holbourne of Menstrie Museum, that today houses various artistic displays.

23

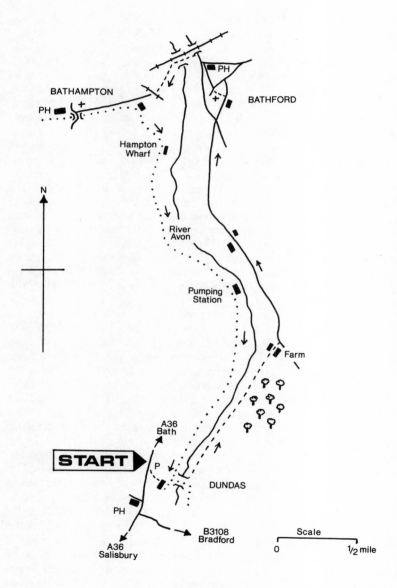

BATHAMPTON

PH

BATHFORD

PH

Hampton
Wharf

N

River
Avon

Pumping
Station

Farm

START

A36
Bath

P

DUNDAS

PH

A36
Salisbury

B3108
Bradford

Scale

0   ½ mile

Claverton, Dundas and the Avon Valley

Introduction: Between Bath and Bradford-on-Avon, the Kennet & Avon Canal passes through the Avon Valley, amidst what is arguably the finest natural landscape along the whole length of the waterway. Steep, wooded hillsides rise for over 400 ft above the valley bottom, hills formed of the golden limestone that was the building material of Georgian Bath. The various means of communication that cling together along the valley floor tell the complete human history of transport from footpaths and rivers, through the canal and railway eras to the modern motor age. This undulating ramble, that avoids the tempting but strenuous climbs to the surrounding hilltops, follows the course of the river Avon from Dundas to Bathampton, before returning by way of the K & A towpath. It is a section of the canal that will linger long in the memory, with its many delights including Hampton Wharf, Claverton Pumping Station, and the junction with the Somerset Coal Canal alongside Dundas Wharf and the magnificent Dundas Aqueduct.

Distance: A 6 mile circuit that includes a potentially muddy riverside path between Dundas and Sheephouse Farm. You would need about 3 hours to complete the walk comfortably. Maps: OS Landranger 172 'Bristol & Bath'; OS Pathfinder ST 66/76 'Bath & Keynsham'.

Refreshments: At Bathford, halfway around the walk, you will pass the Crown Inn. At the end of the circuit, the Viaduct Inn lies just minutes away from Dundas Wharf.

How to get there: Dundas Aqueduct and the K & A Canal lie just below the A36 Bath to Warminster road near Limpley Stoke. A few hundred yards before its junction with the B3108 Bradford-on-Avon road, there is a lay-by on the left-hand side of the A36, alongside the Monkton Combe Garage. Park in the lay-by. (GR 784 626)

The Walk: From Dundas Wharf, follow the towpath in the direction signposted Claverton. Cross the white footbridge to the far side of the waterway where, instead of turning left and actually heading off for Claverton, you turn to the right and cross Dundas Aqueduct. Just before the canal turns sharply to the right to head off for Avoncliff, climb down a series of wooden steps on the left-hand side into the fields alongside the river Avon.

Follow the river downstream, not forgetting to pause and pay suitable homage to the quite magnificent Dundas Aqueduct! In the third field along the river from Dundas, bear right, away from the river's edge, to follow a clear path that leads uphill to Sheephouse Farm. Stiles and yellow arrows guide you through the farmyard to the Conkwell to Bathford minor road.

Turn left at the road, and it is 1½ miles of tarmac through to the A363 and Bathford. The views from this quiet lane are quite superb, and include Claverton village clinging to the hillside, as well as the pumping station down on the river-bank. Everywhere it is stone, the golden Bath stone, that adds a complementary man-made aspect to the natural landscape.

Cross the A363 into Pump Lane and continue to an area of local authority housing on the right-hand side where a road bears the delightful name of Mountain Wood. At this point, you will pass Manor Farm Cottage on the left, beyond which an enclosed path is followed down to Bathford church. Cross the road at the entrance to the church, and take the turning opposite which eventually descends steeply to reach the Crown Inn and the A363. The road leading from the church to the Crown is appropriately named Ostlings Lane, an ostler being a stableman at an inn.

Turn right at the A363, and follow the pavement across By Brook to the railway bridge that carries the main London line. Just this side of the bridge, follow the footpath on the left that climbs up to track level and uses the bridge itself to cross the river Avon.

Once across the river, the path descends to field level where, at a stile, you bear half-right across two open fields to reach a level-crossing across the Bath to Bradford-on-Avon Railway. The red warning signs at the crossing are visible from some distance.

Once across the railway, follow the lane beyond for less than ¼ mile to the K & A Canal. (A brief detour along the towpath to the right will bring you to Bathampton, where the church and the George Inn overlook the waterway.)

The return to Dundas involves following the towpath to the left for close on 3 miles. Hampton Wharf is the first feature along the way, followed in one mile by the outflows from Claverton Pumping Station busily topping up the canal. A short detour down the lane just beyond these outflows will bring you to the pumping station itself. Beyond Claverton, it is another 1½ miles of towpath back to Dundas, the waterway being a paradise for various types of wildfowl. In addition to the ubiquitous species like mallard, coot and moorhen, the quiet rambler may well take a kingfisher or heron by surprise.

Historical Notes

Dundas Aqueduct is a fine construction of local Bath Stone, completed in about 1800 in the Doric style. The central semi-circular arch, some 64 ft in diameter, carries the K & A across the river Avon, whilst the smaller outside arches carry the waterway across a footpath and the Bristol to Southampton railway respectively. The aqueduct is 150 yards in length and enjoys a picturesque location where fields and woodland sweep down to the Avon from the surrounding hillsides. The inscription on the southern side of Dundas explains the origin of its name:

'To Charles Dundas
Chairman of the Kennet and Avon Canal Company
From its commencement
The proprietors
Mindful of his important services
And his unremitting exertions through a period of XL years
Gratefully erected this tablet
A.D. MDCCCXXVIII'

At the eastern end of the aqueduct, a double-track self-acting tram-road, 700 yards in length and with a 1-in-5 gradient, originally came down the hillside from Conkwell Quarry. The quality of the stone was poor, and the quarry's life short. A local, almost unbelievable, tale tells how boys from the local Monkton Combe School at one time dared each other to cycle across the aqueduct on the 4 ft wide cornices that overhang the river from the solid parapets either side of the waterway. A truly frightening thought!

Alongside the aqueduct is **Dundas Wharf**. The setting, with is stone warehouse, wharfside crane and toll office, is particularly evocative of a former age. The wharf marks the junction of the K & A with the **Somerset Coal Canal**, that ran through to the mines around Paulton and Radstock. An Act of 1794 authorised the 'making of a navigable canal, with certain rail-ways and stone-roads, from several collieries in the County of Somerset to communicate with the intended Kennet and Avon Canal.' The SCC was working through to Paulton by 1805, and by 1858 was carrying 165,000 tons of coal per annum. With the opening of a parallel railway, tonnage had fallen to just 20,000 tons by 1890, and in just three years the canal had gone into liquidation. Today, the first 400 yards of the SCC have been restored as moorings, making Dundas almost as busy a location as in its commercial heyday. (Readers interested in exploring the SCC will find a relevant walk in my *Avon Rambles* book, also published by Countryside Books.)

Bathford was the site of an ancient ford across By Brook, close to its confluence with the river Avon, a crossing since replaced by a stone bridge. The village, with its many fine houses built of the local limestone, clings to the steep slopes of Bathford Hill. St Swithin's church has been described as an 'uninspired Victorian effort', but its older features, including a Norman doorway, a 13th century font and a Jacobean pulpit, certainly make it worth a visit. Some of the village's more impressive 18th century houses, including Eagle House designed by John Wood the Elder, the architect of Georgian Bath, are sited around the church.

St Nicholas' Church, Bathampton, with its distinctive red clock face, contains effigies that date back as far as the 11th century. However, the building is mainly the result of rebuilding by Ralph Allen in the 1750s, a project undertaken after he married into the family of the local manor. Of more interest than the building, perhaps, are two notable characters whose remains lie buried within the church. Viscount du Barry, nephew of Louis XV's mistress, was buried here in the late 18th century following a mortal wound inflicted in the last legal duel fought on English soil. His victor was actually a friend, one Colonel Rice, and the duel on nearby Bathampton Down was the result of a quarrel. Also resting within Bathampton church are the remains of Admiral Arthur Phillip, the first Governor of New South Wales, who had carried out the initial colonisation of Australia. A chapel to his memory was furnished by the Australian Government, following appeals to the Australians in 1967 by the vicar, the Reverend Gordon Spencer, for a more fitting memorial to one of the modern nation's founding fathers.

Hampton Wharf, on the K & A, lies at the foot of a former mile long self-acting tramroad, that ran from Bathampton Quarry, high on the hilltops. Opened in 1808, the stone that was carried down the 1-in-5 incline was subsequently used for construction work on the canal. Today the wharf provides handsome moorings and services for the pleasure craft that use the waterway, the whole scene overlooked by one of Rennie's original canal cottages.

Claverton Pumping Station lifted water from the Avon into the canal's 9 mile pound between Bradford-on-Avon and Bath. The pump was powered by a pair of coupled breast water-wheels, each 11 ft 6 in wide and 15 ft 6 in in diameter. John Rennie was responsible for their installation, with the station coming into operation in 1813. Other than during modification by Harvey's of Hayle in 1843, the pumping station was working through to 1952, when damage forced its abandonment. This derelict monument to a former age was rescued by a band of volunteers in 1979, who took eight years to complete their restoration programme. The pumping station is open to the public on Sundays during the summer, and is occasionally fully operational. Water is still pumped into the K & A at Claverton, only today's electric pumps somehow fail to match the splendour of their predecessor!

Avoncliff and Bradford-on-Avon

Introduction: East of Dundas, the Kennet & Avon Canal continues through the steep-sided and heavily wooded Avon Valley before reaching another fine aqueduct at Avoncliff. From this secluded hamlet, the waterway passes through the Barton Farm Country Park before reaching Bradford-on-Avon, widely recognised as one of England's most attractive small towns. The local townscape has been described as 'Bath in miniature' on account of the many fine buildings shaped and fashioned from the local stone. These range from the magnificent Saxon church and 14th century tithe barn, through to a canal wharf of some distinction. The circuit explores the towpath between Avoncliff and Bradford, as well as embracing the riverbank and woodland scenery in and around the country park.

Distance: A none too strenuous 4 mile circuit, that would make a very leisurely half-day excursion. Maps: OS Landranger 173 'Swindon & Devizes'; OS Pathfinder ST 86/96 'Melksham' and ST 85/95 'Westbury & Trowbridge'.

Refreshments: Alongside the canal at Avoncliff is the popular Cross Guns public house, although teetotallers may prefer the nearby tea-room. Bradford-on-Avon has a wide selection of good inns and cafes for visitors.

How to get there: Bradford-on-Avon lies on the A363 Bath to Trowbridge road. Alongside the well signposted railway station is a large free carpark. (GR 824 607)

The Walk: From the railway station, walk to the far end of the carpark and follow the path alongside the river Avon that passes under the railway bridge. Follow the river bank for over ½ mile, through the Barton Farm Country Park, until the tarmac path climbs

30

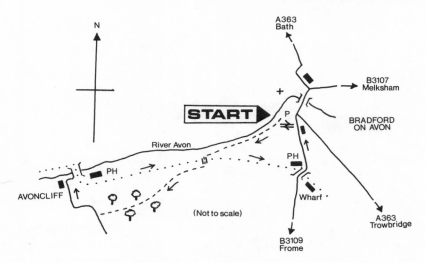

to join the K & A Canal alongside a swingbridge. Cross the bridge, turn right and follow a footpath alongside the far bank of the canal. The path ends at a stile.

Cross this stile into an open field and follow the right-hand hedgerow until you reach a second stile. In the next field, bear half-left to climb the hillside ahead, aiming for one final stile that leads into Becky Addy Woods. For the next ½ mile, the footpath passes through shady woodland, the right-of-way well defined, before emerging onto a quiet country lane.

Turn right, and head downhill into the fascinating hamlet of Avoncliff, dominated by its magnificent aqueduct. Follow the lane beneath the aqueduct to emerge in front of the Cross Guns public house. Thirsts quenched, follow the canal as it passes behind the Cross Guns to wend its way towards Bradford-on-Avon. In a little over a mile, the towpath passes the town's quite magnificent tithe barn, before reaching a hump-back bridge and the B3109 Frome road. Beyond the bridge is Bradford Wharf – well worth the short detour.

To return to the town centre, turn left at the B3109 and it is just ¼ mile of pavement walking to reach the station carpark.

31

Historical Notes

Bradford-on-Avon was historically a 'broad ford' through the river Avon. The town's wealth was founded upon the woollen trade, with any number of mills being powered by the waters of the Avon. The local cloth manufacturers invested their riches in many fine stone buildings, all lovingly fashioned from mellowed Bath stone. The town quite literally rises in steep tiers of dwellings above the Avon, an unforgettable sight when illuminated by the fading rays of an early autumn sunset. A fine stone bridge crosses the river, with two arches that date back as far as the 14th century. In the middle of the bridge is a small lock-up, which housed prisoners overnight whilst en route to gaols in Bristol and Salisbury.

Bradford's Saxon church is one of the best preserved examples in the country, and was only discovered by chance! For many years, it lay hidden amongst a jumble of later buildings, its original function lost in the mists of time. It was only in 1856, when a local vicar happened to look across the roof tops and espy a mysterious cross, that St Laurence once again became a place of worship. It is a plain building, as high as it is long, with very little by way of internal embellishment. In many ways, the beauty of the Saxon church lies in this very simplicity. The other sites in and around Bradford-on-Avon, such as the tithe barn, the Shambles, Dutch Barton and the Hall, have filled many a weighty tome. I can but recommend that the interested visitor invest in a copy of the town guide.

Avoncliff is an isolated hamlet tucked away in one of the least accessible corners of the Avon Valley. Dominating the settlement is the 110 yard long aqueduct that carries the K & A across the valley. Constructed of the local Bath stone, its essential features are three arches, a solid parapet and balustraded ends. Close study of the stonework will reveal an interesting selection of masons' marks. The prominent sagging of the centre arch actually occurred during the construction of the aqueduct in 1798, and in no way signifies a dangerous structure! At the southern end of the aqueduct, alongside the Cross Guns, the wide canal basin represents the site of Avoncliff Wharf. Much stone from the quarries at Upper Westwood, a village high on the hilltops, would have been transhipped at the wharf. The railway between Bradford-on-Avon and Bath, opened in 1857, runs beneath the aqueduct and serves Avoncliff Halt, surely one of the smallest stations on the BR network. The towpath along the western side of the canal once carried a siding of the Upper Westwood Quarry Railway, that ran to an exchange siding alongside the main line. The only evidence remaining of this link, however, is in dusty old photographs! The weir upstream of the aqueduct originally powered two local flock mills. Both still stand at either side of the weir, but in contrasting states of repair. The dereliction of the left-hand mill is in marked contrast to the handsome conversion that has turned its partner into a fine residence.

Bradford Wharf is in fact something of a misnomer, for the town at one time could boast two wharves: Frome Road Wharf above the lock, Lower Wharf below. Bradford Lock was, until 1976, the deepest lock on the K & A, with a rise/fall of 10 ft 3 in. It lost this claim to fame that year when locks 8 and 9 in Bath were amalgamated to form Bath Deep Lock as part of a road improvement scheme in the city. It was somewhere in the vicinity of Bradford Wharf that a second claim to fame arose. It was here in October 1794 that the first turf was cut to commence work on the canal's construction. The Wharf today presents a fine example of canal architecture. Alongside the lock chamber is an original warehouse, accompanied by one of only two dry docks on the whole waterway. The other example is to be found at the summit of the Caen Hill locks in Devizes. The dock is made 'dry' by the removal of a plug when the chamber has been sealed off by the use of wooden 'stop' planks. West of Bradford, the canal bed was regularly 'puddled' with clay to stem frequent leaks in the notorious 'dry pound'. A hundred yards east of the Wharf lies the site of a clay 'farm', where this vital material for the K & A was extracted.

Barton Farm Country Park is a narrow strip of meadowland bounded by the river Avon to the north and the K & A Canal to the south. It runs for over a mile between Bradford-on-Avon and Avoncliff, and is a haven for walking, coarse fishing and bird-watching. Herons and kingfishers are common visitors to this watery paradise. At the eastern end of the Park lies Barton Farm itself. The complex of buildings includes, in addition to the farmhouse, a tithe barn, various outbuildings and a packhorse bridge. Collectively, these buildings provide a fine example of medieval architecture. This was once but a small corner of the rich demesne of Shaftesbury Abbey. The tithe barn is now an English Heritage property, whilst the various outbuildings house an assortment of craft workshops.

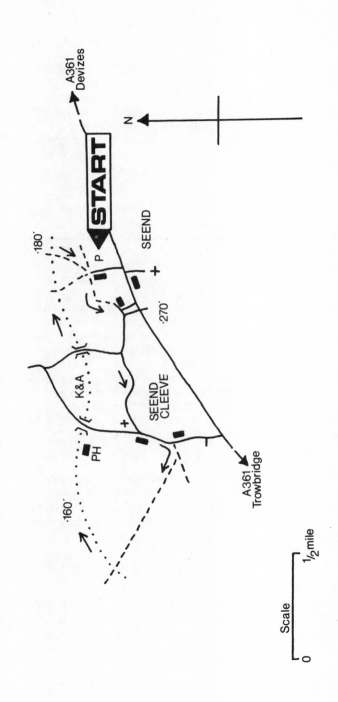

Seend and Seend Cleeve

Introduction: Between Bradford-on-Avon and Devizes, the landscape is generally flat and unspectacular. Hereabouts, the canal borders the southern boundary of the North Wiltshire Clay Vale, and the limestone hills around Bath and Dundas are but a distant memory. It is almost as if the Kennet & Avon Canal is pausing for breath before the rigours of the Caen Hill Locks just a few miles distant. The villages of Seend and Seend Cleeve, midway between Trowbridge and Devizes, straddle a small ridge of hills overlooking this section of the canal. The contours rise to little more than the 300 ft mark, but it is the contrast with the Vale that creates the interest. Along the waterway lie several attractions, including a selection of locks, a canalside inn and the site of an old iron-works, whilst in Seend itself are some fine houses whose origins lie in the wealth created by the local cloth industry.

Distance: A straightforward 3½ mile circuit through gently undulating countryside, this walk would make a pleasant half-day excursion. Maps: OS Landranger 173 'Swindon & Devizes'; OS Pathfinder ST 86/96 'Melksham'.

Refreshments: Conveniently located just over halfway around the walk is the Barge Inn, with an idyllic canalside situation. The Barge serves Wadworths Ales, brewed in nearby Devizes, and concocts delicious home-made meals.

How to get there: Seend lies midway between Trowbridge and Devizes on the main A361 road. When travelling from Trowbridge through the village, look out for Rusty Lane on the left-hand side, a turning that is signposted as leading to the 'Village Halls'. Park at the end of the lane opposite Seend Social Club. (GR 943 613)

The Walk: Continue along the track to the north of Seend Social Club for just a few yards to a five-way junction of paths. Turn left to follow the path across the hilltop, with fine views across the Avon Vale towards Melksham. The path eventually becomes hemmed in with a good selection of blackberry bushes before joining an access road into a small housing development. Turn right, continue to a road junction and turn right again. In 300 yards, the 'main' road bears to the right downhill towards the Melksham to Devizes road, whilst our route lies along the minor road ahead signposted to Seend Cleeve. This is a pleasant hillside settlement, where the old and the new blend harmoniously. The abundance of traditional brick and slate building materials are a sure sign that Bath stone country is now well behind us. Keep on the main road through the village, avoiding any tempting side turns, bearing left at a junction just beyond an old chapel.

In 200 yards, just before Rew Farm, turn right into Park Lane. This access road soon becomes a stony track before hitting open country at a gateway a short distance ahead. Turn right at this gateway, and follow the path that runs alongside the right-hand hedgerow through the next couple of fields. Beyond this, continue across the middle of two smaller fields, keeping the same direction, until you reach Seend Park Swing Bridge and the K & A.

Cross the canal, and follow the towpath for close on 2 miles in an easterly direction (ie, to the right) until you reach the second swing-bridge beyond Seend Top Lock, number 21. This is Sells Green Swing Bridge, the site of the former Scott's Wharf. Along this section of towpath, you will pass the five locks that make up the Seend flight as well as the bargees' watering hole, the Barge Inn. In the fields alongside lock 19, just beyond the Barge, the humps are all that remain of the former Seend Iron Works (see historical notes).

Cross Sells Green Swing Bridge, and bear half-right to climb to a stile in the far right-hand corner of the field ahead. In the next field, climb to the far right-hand corner again to reach the five-way junction encountered at the beginning of the walk. This time continue straight ahead to return to the parking area.

Should you wish to explore Holy Cross church, continue along Rusty Lane to the main A361, turn right and the drive leading to the church is the first turning on the left.

Historical Notes

The Kennet & Avon Canal: Between Seend Park and Sells Green Swing Bridges, the canal climbs a 38 ft rise by means of locks numbers 17 to 21. Located between locks 18 and 19 is the Barge Inn which, with the adjoining stone cottage, mark the site of Seend Wharf. The inn provided both liquid refreshment for the bargees and stabling for their horses. Sells Green Swing Bridge, where the walk leaves the canal to return to Seend, marks the site of Scott's Wharf, whilst a little further east lies the site of Wragg's Wharf. Until 1898, the Wragg family used to operate a pair of narrow boats between Dunkerton, on the Somerset Coal Canal, and Seend, carrying fuel for the local villagers. Traffic ceased in that year with the official closure of the SCC. Coal was the 'staple diet' of the K & A, enabling the Canal Company to pay dividends that averaged just over 3 per cent between 1824 and 1841 when the Great Western Railway opened.

Seend Iron Works: At Seend, iron-ore deposits associated with the ferruginous sands of the Lower Greensand, gave rise to a 19th century iron industry. Prior to this time, the ore had been worked by local smiths, one commentator noting that 'it could be smelted in the forge of the local blacksmith with greater ease than the ore of the Forest of Dean'. In 1857, the site of the ore deposits – the land alongside lock 19 – was acquired by the Great Western Iron Ore Smelting Company. Two blast furnaces were erected, together with tramways to link with both the K & A and the nearby Devizes Railway.

The works struggled financially, as is evident by the steady succession of owners who picked up the pieces from former bankrupts! Typical of the various owners were William and Samuel Malcolm of Glasgow, who began working the ironstone in 1870. It was not long before they were employing 300 men on the site, producing 300 tons of iron each week. By 1873, however, the Messrs Malcolm were facing hard times at Seend and the firm crashed with liabilities of £350,000. The last commercial operators on the site, the Westbury and Seend Ore and Oxide Company, commenced a straightforward ore mining operation in 1905. The ironstone was transported to South Wales for processing. The falling demand for iron after the First World War, though, spelled the end of all operations at Seend.

Today, several relics of this short chapter in the village's history remain. The site of the works is now pasture, although the grassy

37

hummocks represent former spoil heaps; to the north of the Barge Inn, the raised embankment that carried a tramline to the Devizes railway is clearly visible; the terrace of cottages north of Seend Wharf Bridge are former iron workers' houses; whilst in Seend Cleeve, the walk passes the entrance to Ferrum Towers, home of the former ironmaster.

Seend: The 17th century antiquary John Aubrey spoke highly of Seend when he commented 'I know not of any small village that has so many well-built houses'. As with many other settlements in the West of England, it was the local woollen industry that was the source of the wealth responsible for their creation. The establishment of a weaving industry in Seend has been attributed to Henry VII, who encouraged a company of Flemish clothiers to come to England. Seend was a perfectly sensible place to settle for, in addition to the local flocks of sheep, the nearby Semington Brook provided an ample source of water power. The Flemish clothiers stayed long enough to leave their mark in the form of many fine houses built along the village High Street.

A walled driveway between the 18th century Manor and the grounds of Seend House leads to Holy Cross church. The north aisle of the church was also a product of the wealth created by the cloth industry, the 14th century clothier John Stokys being instrumental in its construction. Brasses to Stokys and his wife adorn the west wall, beneath a window with the clothier's shears and scissors carved into the moulding of the arch. The church enjoys a beautiful location, sitting proudly on the brow of a hill overlooking the clay vale, with the scarp slope of Salisbury Plain rising in the distance. It possesses a fine pinnacled tower, beautiful clerestory windows and battlemented parapets. The external embellishments also include a grotesque selection of gargoyles, where lions, dragons and an ape are the companions of a pair of bagpipe players!

Devizes and The Caen Hill 'Locks'

Introduction: 'Devizes Devizes is full of surprises' goes a local saying. Perhaps the biggest surprise of all is the incredible staircase of locks, some 16 in all, that carry the Kennet & Avon Canal the height of Caen Hill to the west of the town. Devizes itself is a picturesque market town, full of quaint alleys and red-brick dwellings that focus upon the Market Place. This walk is an attempt to link these two strands of the town's history. A short town-trail is followed by an extensive exploration of Caen Hill and the canalside environment. As an added attraction, the footpath across the fields to the foot of Caen Hill brings with it fine views of Roundway Hill, the dramatic escarpment to the north of the town where the chalk downlands meet the clay vale.

Distance: A 4 mile circuit that includes a few sections of potentially muddy towpath. The walk itself could easily be completed in two hours but canal enthusiasts will need to allow plenty of time to admire the flight of locks. Maps: OS Landranger 173 'Swindon & Devizes'; OS Pathfinder ST 86/96 'Melksham' and 1185 'Devizes & Marlborough'.

Refreshments: Just beyond the summit of the Caen Hill Staircase, the Black Horse Inn backs onto the canal. The Black Horse serves traditional ales and home-cooked meals. In Devizes town centre are a good selection of refreshment amenities.

How to get there: Devizes lies on the A361 Trowbridge to Swindon road. Approaching from the west, the A361 bears left at a mini-roundabout alongside Wadworth's Brewery. In a few hundred yards, the Wharf Centre is signposted along a turning on the left-hand side. There is ample parking alongside the Wharf. (GR 004 617)

39

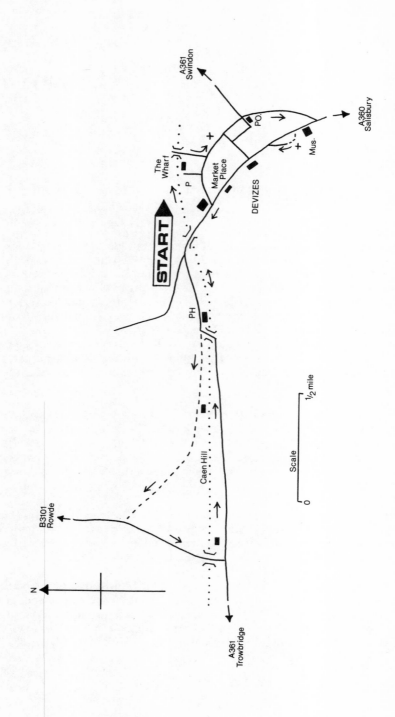

The Walk: Follow Couch Lane, the road behind the Wharf Centre, down to New Park Street. Turn left, follow the pavement alongside this busy road past St Mary's church, continue straight ahead at the nearby roundabout and carry on to the junction with Sidmouth Street. Using the pedestrian crossings, cross over to Sheep Street. Continue along Sheep Street for another 400 yards to its junction with Long Street, where you turn right. The traditional red-brick buildings that are a feature of Devizes are amply present in this fine street. You will soon pass Devizes Museum on the left-hand side, home of the Wiltshire Archaeological and Natural History Society. The extensive local displays are excellent, and well worth an hour of anybody's time.

Just beyond the museum, turn left into St John's churchyard and the parish church. Follow a path around to the right of the yard, where a gateway leads through to St John's Court. Beyond St John's Court, with the town hall and lock-up on the right-hand side, continue straight ahead along St John's Street and through to the Market Place. Market-day is Thursday, when the square is filled with the noise of traders, but on any day this is rather an attractive setting.

Continue across the Market Place and onto Northgate Street, with the red-brick Wadworth's Brewery on your right. This monument to 19th century industrial architecture is as attractive in its own way as the Listed buildings around the Market Place. In less than 200 yards, the road crosses the K & A. Follow the steps on the left down to the towpath, and head westwards towards the top of the Caen Hill flight. It is not long before the canal passes under the A361 to reach the top lock.

At this point, we bid the canal a temporary farewell. Leave the towpath by an exit on the left-hand side BEFORE passing under the road-bridge. Cross over *the top* of the K & A and take the first turning on the left, an access road that leads into the BWB maintenance depot. Continue along this access road which runs parallel to, but slightly below, the canal, passing to the right of the BWB yard. Where the path divides at a small fenced in compound, fork to the right along a turning that brings you to an untidy jumble of agricultural buildings – something to do with pigs and poultry at the last count!

The well defined path passes behind a long wooden shed and then follows the hedgerow that borders the lock pounds, before bearing to the right across open fields to join the B3101 Rowde road. The magnificent scarp slopes a mile or two to the north mark the boundary of the Wessex Downs and the Avon's clay vale. The most

41

prominent hill is Roundway Hill, site of Oliver's Castle, an ancient hillfort.

Turn left at the road, and carefully follow this sometimes busy lane for ¼ mile to a humped-back bridge at the foot of the Caen Hill Staircase. The view uphill of the 16 consecutive locks is one of the wonders of the waterways world, and will no doubt cost you a small fortune in film printing and processing!

Make your way down to the towpath, which is your constant companion for the 2 mile return journey to the wharf. The first section of this leg will, of course, be dominated by the lock chambers and their neighbouring pounds. Just ¼ mile from the wharf, where the K & A passes beneath the A361 before reaching Kennet Lock, the towpath changes to the north bank of the canal, whilst back at the wharf a stone bridge will return you to the 'right' side of the canal for your car.

Upon your return, a visit to the Wharf Centre is almost obligatory, with the converted granary now housing the K & A Canal Trust's headquarters, together with a shop and exhibition area.

Historical Notes

With **Devizes** sitting squarely at the point where the manors of Rowde, Cannings and Potterne met, its name is clearly self-explanatory. *Ad divisas* is simply the Latin phrase for 'at the boundaries'. Bishop Roger of Salisbury built a castle here in 1120, which was at one time occupied by Queen Matilda during her conflict with her cousin Stephen over successional rights to the throne. The town was granted a charter in 1141, and was subsequently honoured with several royal connections. During the Civil War, the Royalists held Devizes following their victory at the nearby Battle of Roundway. Their occupancy was, however, shortlived for in 1645 Cromwell captured part of Devizes and destroyed its castle. It was rebuilt in the 19th century in the Norman style, but has served merely as a private residence since that date.

The town is blessed with an abundance of fine buildings that include St John's church, the Town Hall, the Market Cross, the Corn Exchange and the Bear Hotel. Being at the centre of a rich agricultural community, it is no surprise to find these buildings grouped in and around the large Market Place. St John's church has been described as 'a pleasing blend of heavy Norman and later more ornate 15th-century work', whose precise origins date back to circa 1130. The chancel, the tower and the transepts are widely held to be some of the most detailed Norman work in Britain. Architecture aside, the churchyard is worth visiting if only to glimpse the now very private castle.

Almost the best known aspect of Devizes is **Wadworth's Brewery**. Henry Wadworth constructed the fine red-brick premises on their present site in 1885. Wadworths rapidly expanded, and through a process of merger and acquisition became one of the West of England's largest brewers. The Bromham Brewery, for example, was taken over in 1896, whilst the Estcourt Brewery followed in 1903. Parallel to this merger activity, Wadworths were rapidly buying up local inns and hotels to guarantee a market for their fine ales. Until 1976, the original 19th century equipment was still in use at the Northgate Street premises, and even today the brewing methods are largely the same as in Henry Wadworth's day. The ales, too, have long been held in high esteem by serious drinkers. The '6X' and 'Old Timer' brews have been known to turn many a strong pair of Wiltshire legs to a quivering mass of jelly!

The **Caen Hill staircase** of 16 locks are the centre-piece of a longer flight of 29 locks that carry the K & A up a rise of 234 ft on the 2 mile western approach to Devizes Wharf. West of Caen Hill lie the seven locks of the Foxhangers Flight, whilst above Caen Hill there are six further locks before the wharf is reached. The awesome Caen Hill staircase is paralleled by a number of side pounds, vast reservoirs that ensure a steady supply of water to the locks. Such a major engineering feat as Caen Hill obviously provided the key to the final restoration of the K & A. It was with the royal opening, or rather reopening, of the staircase in the summer of 1990, that a through link between the Thames and the Avon was once again open to boaters. Ironically, it was the completion of Caen Hill in 1810 that meant that the waterway was originally fully operational throughout its length. Between 1802 and 1810, a temporary horse-drawn tramway linked the foot and the summit of the incline, and hence the western and eastern sections of the canal. Millions of bricks were used in the construction of the chambers, the clay pit lying to the south of locks 29 to 35 providing the necessary gault clay. This was the largest exposure of this material in Central-Southern England, the deposit being so extensive that it also enabled enough bricks to be produced to build the Bruce Tunnel south of Marlborough. A question that always

43

presents itself to visitors is how long it would take to pass through the Caen Hill staircase. The record was supposedly set by a JT Ferris, who ran a 45 ton wideboat between the Colthrop Mills near Newbury and Bristol. He is reported to have worked his way up the flight on one occasion in a mere 2½ hours! Had he been travelling at night, his passage would have been assisted by the gaslights on Caen Hill that permitted 24 hour working. There was even a K & A gasworks to the west of the cottage alongside lock 26, but in order to make such a venture profitable, an extra shilling was charged to use the locks after dark!

Devizes Wharf, with its wharfinger's house and warehouse, presents a handsome canalside scene. The crane belonging to the warehouse has long since disappeared, although the building itself has been sympathetically restored and houses the excellent Wharf Theatre. The original trade at the wharf was dominated by coal, carried to the K & A by means of the Somerset Coal Canal. Stone, brick, timber and various agricultural items made up the rest of the trade. It was with the arrival of the canal in Devizes that Bath stone began to appear in the town, providing an alternative to the local red brick when it came to building materials. End onto the canal at the wharf lies a building that in its time has served as a granary and a bonded warehouse. Today, it houses the K & A Canal Trust's headquarters, where various displays relating to the canal are housed. The exhibits focus, quite rightly, on the characters who made the canal what it was – the navvies and the engineers, the boatmen and the lock-keepers, who operated the waterway. One notable local operator was William Dickenson, whose service between Devizes and Avonmouth Docks west of Bristol was so reliable that it continued to find customers long after the arrival of the railway.

Bishops Cannings
and the Wansdyke

Introduction: East of Devizes, the Kennet & Avon Canal follows a meandering course across the flat and fertile Vale of Pewsey. From Kennet Lock in Devizes through to Wootton Rivers is a distance of some 15 miles without a single lock. This must have come as welcome relief to the bargees after the 29 locks that had to be negotiated in just 2¼ miles to the west of Devizes Wharf! The scenery in the Vale is far from uninteresting, however. To the north rise the North Wessex Downs, a massive chalk upland that covers large areas of Wiltshire and Berkshire. The highest point on the downs, Tan Hill, rises to a height of 964 ft just a mile or two north of the canal at Allington. This particular stretch of the downs is also crossed by the Wansdyke, an ancient line of defence that is characterised by a massive 25 ft high bank. This is the area explored in this lengthy ramble. A 4 mile towpath walk, a sharp climb onto the hills, and a generous section of the Wansdyke to the west of Tan Hill make up this substantial ramble amidst some of the best natural landscape in Wiltshire.

Distance: This 10 mile circuit that includes a climb onto Wiltshire's highest tract of downland would need a full day to complete. Maps: OS Landranger 173 'Swindon & Devizes'; OS Pathfinder 1185 'Devizes & Marlborough'.

Refreshments: At the end of the walk you will find welcome sustenance in the Crown Inn at Bishops Cannings. Any refreshments en route will have to be carried with you, which is no bad idea given the fine viewpoints that exist on the hilltops.

How to get there: Follow the A361 north-eastwards from Devizes towards Swindon. Three miles out of Devizes turn right along an

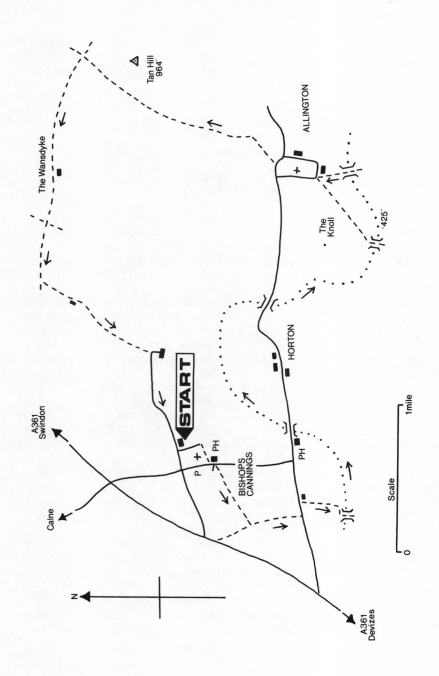

unclassified road signposted to Bishops Cannings. Park in the road alongside the village's prominent church. (GR 038 642)

The Walk: From Bishops Cannings church, head southwards along the road, past the Crown Inn and onto a right turn signposted 'The Estate Yard'. At this junction, a telephone box stands alongside a gateway. Cross the gate and, in the field beyond, aim for the top left-hand corner where you cross a wooden barrier in the barbed-wire fence into the next field. Turn right, and follow the right-hand field boundary across two fields until, just before some overhead power lines, the field path crosses a stile to join a track.

Turn left, and follow the track for ¼ mile to the Devizes road. The views from this track are far-ranging, and include Etchilhampton Hill a mile or two to the south, Devizes to the west and Tan Hill to the east, all part of an archetypal Wiltshire landscape of chalk hills overlooking the clay vale.

Turn left at the road and, in just 100 yards, right into the field just before some wooden farm buildings. A well-defined track passes around the edge of this field to Laywood Bridge and the K & A Canal.

Follow the towpath in an easterly direction (counting the bridges) for close on 4 miles, as the canal follows a meandering course across the Vale of Pewsey. One very marked loop in the waterway's course occurs as the K & A skirts the southern slopes of an area of high ground known as 'The Knoll'. To ensure that you leave the towpath at the appropriate point, count the traditional red-brick bridges: ¾ mile on from Laywood Bridge is Horton Bridge, alongside the Bridge Inn; in another 1½ miles, Horton Chain Bridge carries the Devizes road across the K & A; in another mile, Allington Bridge carries a lane to the hamlet of the same name. Half a mile beyond Allington Bridge brings you to a swing-bridge.

Cross to the north bank of the canal and follow a grass track into Allington. Where this track meets the road alongside Allington House, continue straight ahead. A short distance after passing Bethel Strict Baptist chapel on your right-hand side, you will join the Devizes to Alton Barnes road.

Turn right, and follow this road for a few yards to a point where it bears to the right. At this point, leave the road and turn left onto a bridlepath that heads northwards towards the magnificent chalk downlands. This bridlepath is followed for 1½ miles as it climbs the chalk escarpment, with Tan Hill on your right-hand side. On the hilltop, after crossing a number of cattle grids, you will see the unmistakable shape of the Wansdyke crossing your path. The choice of location for this ancient fortification of ditch and bank, that acted as a defence against attack from the north, is clear to see – any invasions from that direction could be spotted long in advance. The views are far-ranging and defy description!

Follow the Wansdyke westwards (i.e. to the left), past a complex of farm buildings, to a point 1½ miles distant where the fortification begins to climb the hillside. Here a farm track, that has run a parallel course to the Wansdyke on its right-hand side, crosses your path and heads to the brow of the hill on the left. It then descends towards Bishops Cannings – your ultimate destination.

Follow the track down to Easton Farm and turn right along the lane towards the village. Back in Bishops Cannings, turn left just beyond the school into The Street, followed in 200 yards by a right turn into Church Walk. This path leads into the churchyard, at the far side of which lies the road and your vehicle.

Historical Notes

Bishops Cannings, a pleasing blend of thatch and brick, sits nestled in a fold of the nearby chalk downs. All approaches to the village are dominated by the 130 ft high spire of St Mary the Virgin church, in many ways a replica in miniature of Salisbury cathedral. Both of these religious buildings are cruciform in layout, and are noted for their fine spires. The similarities should come as no surprise for the Bishops of Salisbury owned the local manorial estates from before Domesday through to 1858, when the land was sold to the Crown. The nave arcade and the porch testify to Late Norman influences in architectural styles, whilst the lancet windows introduce Early English designs. The spire itself was a later 15th century addition. Within the church, various artefacts will undoubtedly catch the eye. These include a Jacobean holy table, a 17th century alms box and a penitential chair. The seat of penance is decorated with unusual hand paintings on its back panel, and carries various Latin inscriptions that speak quite naturally of sin and death! The church organ is another item of some interest. It was donated to St Mary the Virgin in 1809 by one William Bayley. Bayley was one of the village's more famous sons, having sailed the world with Captain Cook.

The Kennet & Avon Canal between Laywood Bridge and Allington follows a meandering course across the western end of the Vale of Pewsey, keeping just below the 450 ft contour. With the Vale being a relatively flat landscape, the 15 miles between Devizes and Wootton Rivers was devoid of any locks. The few areas of high ground, such as the 529 ft summit of the Knoll, simply meant a deviation from the straight and narrow! The Vale was always fertile farmland, whose arable crops formed a marked contrast with the sheep grazing on the nearby hills. Such a sparsely populated district gave rise to little trade, making wharves almost as unnecessary as locks. With little by way of canal architecture to catch the eye, it is the natural landscape that will obviously appeal. A sleepy section of the canal, amidst a rural backwater, all set against a magnificent backdrop of chalk hills, it must have seemed the perfect idyll to the sweat-sodden bargee who had just navigated his way through the Caen Hill locks!

Tan Hill, the highest point in Wiltshire at 964 ft above sea-level, lies just to the east of the bridlepath that climbs onto the Downs above Allington. This is one of the highest points in Southern England, beaten by only Leith Hill (965 ft) on the North Downs and Walbury Hill (974 ft) on the Hampshire Downs. One sharp-eyed traveller once assured his readers that he had espied the spire of Salisbury Cathedral, some 20 miles to the south, from these hilltops. I have yet to be convinced! Tan Hill itself is a corruption of St Anne's Hill, and was the site of an annual fair held on St Anne's Day, July 26th, each year. The main business of the day was trade in livestock, particularly sheep, although as a social gathering in the local agricultural calendar it must have been quite some occasion.

The Wansdyke: This linear frontier of bank-and-ditch was built in the 6th or 7th century AD by the Britons, to act as a defence against invading pagan Saxons. It was probably successful in achieving this aim since no pagan Saxon burials have been found south of its line. Its course can be traced from south of Bristol out onto these Downs south of Marlborough. One commentator speculates that it may have marked the one-time boundary of Wessex. Walking the course of the Wansdyke high on these hills has been described as 'one of the most spectacular experiences in British field archaeology'. You will surely echo this comment having explored what is a particularly evocative and atmospheric part of our landscape.

Wilcot Wide Water
and Knap Hill

Introduction: East of Bishops Cannings and Allington (Walk 8), the Kennet & Avon Canal continues on its journey across the Vale of Pewsey. This is still the 15 mile pound between Devizes and Wootton Rivers, where the absence of locks meant continuing relief for the bargees after the rigours of Caen Hill. The major interest to canal lovers will be the ornate landscaping of the K & A as it passes through the grounds of Wilcot Manor. The landowner insisted that the waterway be formed into an ornamental lake – known as Wilcot Wide Water – whose approach was announced by the highly decorative Ladies Bridge. The North Wessex Downs continue to dominate the landscape to the north, where the Alton Barnes white horse is a feature of note. The relatively strenuous circuit embraces both the gentle canal towpath and the rather more rigorous climb onto Draycot Hill and Knap Hill, high downland terrain.

Distance: A 9 mile circuit that includes a height difference of some 500 ft between the K & A in the Vale of Pewsey and the downland slopes around Knap Hill. Maps: OS Landranger sheet 173 'Swindon and Devizes'; OS Pathfinder sheet 1185 'Devizes and Marlborough'.

Refreshments: The Barge Inn at Honey Street will provide welcome sustenance after 6 miles spent exploring the hills, whilst the Golden Swan at Wilcot is a fine inn. Food is available at both hostelries.

How to get there: Wilcot lies 2 miles west of Pewsey, on an unclassified road that leads to Devizes. In the village, park on the roadside in the vicinity of the Golden Swan Inn. (GR 143 612)

The Walk: From the Golden Swan, continue along the Devizes road until it crosses the K & A Canal. Immediately beyond the K & A, turn

50

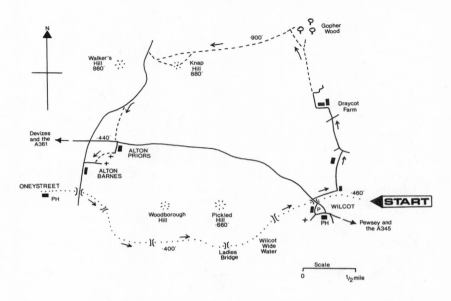

right and follow a lane signposted to East Stowell. This lane runs parallel to the canal for ¼ mile before bearing left, away from the K & A, by a thatched lodge. Follow the lane northwards for ½ mile to a T-junction, turn left and continue along the road ahead for another ½ mile until you come to a crossroads.

Continue straight ahead, following the road signposted to Huish and Draycott. The road bears to the left and the right as it passes through the complex of buildings that make up Draycot Farm, before going downhill. Magnificent views open up ahead of the North Wessex Downs, and the dramatic change from clay vale to chalk downland could not be clearer.

Two hundred yards beyond Draycot Farm, where the road bears to the right, continue straight ahead along a bridlepath beyond a gateway. There is a finger-post at this point, bearing the faint legend 'Milk Hill'. Follow the well defined track for ¾ mile as it climbs Draycott Hill, bringing with it breathtaking views of the chalk escarpment. Just before the hilltop, leave the chalk track to follow a clear grassy path on your left for the final 200 yards of the climb. You emerge onto the breezy heights of the Downs with Knapp Wood just to your right.

51

Turn left, and follow the path beyond a gateway signposted to 'Knap Hill'. Directions for the next 1½ miles are unnecessary since this path literally keeps to the edge of the hilltop, following a well trodden route. There is a hilltop fence at one point where the right-of-way keeps to the left. You eventually reach Knap Hill, site of a Neolithic Camp and various tumuli, where a pause to enjoy the view is almost compulsory. Below lies the Vale of Pewsey, stretching across to the northern edge of Salisbury Plain, Woodborough Hill and Pickled Hill being two prominent hillocks. Further west, the path drops to the Marlborough road, beyond which the prominent hill is Walkers Hill, site of Adam's Grave, an ancient long barrow.

Descend to the Marlborough road, and turn left to follow this relatively quiet byway for ½ mile as it descends the chalk escarpment. Half a mile down the road, an enclosed path heads off on the left-hand side, running parallel to the road. Follow this path (marked on the OS sheets as the Ridge Way) downhill until it joins the Alton to Wilcot road. Cross straight over and follow a cul-de-sac lane to Alton Priors church. The lane ends at an excellent example of a turnstile, with the unfortunately redundant church in the field ahead. The paved path passes to the right of the church, crosses a small footbridge and then bears left to join a lane leading to Alton Barnes Farm and St Mary's Saxon church.

Turn right at the lane – having perhaps made the brief detour to the church first – and left at the road junction you reach in just 200 yards. You are now on the main road through Alton Barnes which, in less than ½ mile, crosses the K&A at Honey Street. Whilst walking along this stretch of road, it is worth looking back to the Downs for a fine view of the Alton Barnes white horse.

On reaching the K&A, the Barge Inn at Honey Street lies 200 yards along the towpath to the right, whilst the return to Wilcot is by way of the towpath to the left (i.e. the east). It is just under 3 miles before you arrive back in Wilcot. In ¾ mile the path switches to the north bank at Woodborough Bridge before continuing under Ladies Bridge to border Wilcot Wide Water. Woodborough Hill and Pickled Hill are our constant companions to the north of the canal throughout this stretch of the walk.

Beyond Wilcot Wide Water, leave the canal at the second over-bridge, adorned with an advertisement for the Golden Swan Inn, turn right and you will very soon return to Wilcot village green and the Swan where the walk began. A right turn at the Green would bring you to the cul-de-sac lane that leads to the village church.

Historical Notes

Wilcot: Brian Woodruffe, in his book entitled *Wiltshire Villages*, places Wilcot alongside such notables as Castle Combe, Lacock and Biddestone in his 'top twenty' Wiltshire villages. The community is centred around an expansive village green, overlooked by estate cottages and thatched dwellings, as well as the Golden Swan Inn. The village church and its neighbouring Manor House lie at the end of a cul-de-sac lane to the south-west of the green. Holy Cross church, whose late Norman chancel arch testifies to its historical origins, was badly damaged by fire in the 19th century. Today's building is largely a rebuilding of 1876. An interesting plaque in the chancel stands as a memory to the son of Admiral Sir John Gore. Gore, the younger, perished at sea in 1835 whilst attempting to rescue a shipmate during a storm. Alongside the church stands the 17th century manor. The history of the estate is much older than this, however, as is evident from an entry in the Domesday Book. Although the manor's vineyards are no more, a glimpse over the boundary wall into the grounds will reveal a fine circular dovecot that dates from 1737.

When the K & A was being cut through Wilcot, tradition maintains that Lady Wroughton of the manor was concerned that it would simply be a blot on the landscape. She would only permit the canal to pass through the estate on the condition that it was formed into a wooded ornamental lake. This has created a most unique feature known as **Wilcot Wide Water**. At Lady Wroughton's insistence, the western approach to the Wide Water was heralded by **Ladies Bridge**, whose overall design resembles in some ways a miniature of the grand aqueducts at Dundas and Avoncliff. Ladies Bridge possesses a marked convex cant, and is noted for its solid parapet which is balustraded at each end. The ornamental stonework adorning the bridge includes lozenges, draped swags, shells and crosses, as well as an inscription that reads 'Erected 1808'. Today's canal traveller will in all probability be much appreciative of Lady Wroughton's whims!

The North Wessex Downs above Wilcot rise to a not inconsiderable 885 ft at Golden Ball Hill. In fact, the whole length of the footpath between Gopher Wood and Knap Hill lies well above the 800 ft contour. Such high ground proved a great attraction for ancient settlers, both for its defensive qualities and its religious aura. **Knap Hill** is the site of a Neolithic Camp, where a bank and ditch enclosed an area of some 4 acres high above the Vale of Pewsey. At the foot of the hill, excavations have revealed substantial pottery fragments of the beaker type entombed in a pair of burial mounds. West of Knap Hill, **Walkers Hill** is the site of Adam's Grave. This late Neolithic long barrow, 200 ft long, 100 ft wide and 20 ft high, provided the archaeologists with several skeletons and a leaf arrow following excavations in the 19th century. This is said to be the site of a battle in AD 592 between the Saxons of Wessex and those of Ceawlin of the Upper Thames Valley. The Anglo Saxon Chronicle records a 'great slaughter' here. Just beyond Adam's Grave is the **Alton Barnes White Horse**. At 650 ft above sea-level, the horse is said to be visible from Old Sarum near Salisbury, some 20 miles away. It was cut in 1812, at the expense of a Mr Robert Pile of Alton Barnes, who paid a journeyman painter £20 to carry out the task. John Thorpe, nick-named Jack the Painter, was foolishly paid in advance. He promptly disappeared! He was later hanged for some unknown crime, leaving Pile the task of finishing the horse himself. Such is the stuff of which legends are made!

Alton Priors and **Alton Barnes** have been described as 'twin villages' – and with their respective churches lying just 200 yards apart, perhaps Siamese twins would be more appropriate! The name 'Alton' is believed to derive from the Saxon word 'awel-tun' which translates to read 'village by the streams'. This is quite apt, with a spring to the north of the villages giving rise to a willow-lined brook that separates Alton Priors from Alton Barnes. It is, in fact, a tributary of what eventually became the Hampshire Avon. The Church of All Saints at Alton Priors enjoys a fine setting quite literally in the middle of a piece of meadow land. Sarsen stone footpaths cross the field to what is now one of the country's growing band of redundant churches. Fortunately, All Saints' is normally unlocked, enabling visitors to enjoy its wide nave, 12th century chancel arch and generally most peaceful interior. The exterior is dominated by the 15th century west tower, which is adorned with a huge sundial. At Alton Barnes, St Mary the Virgin church has been described as 'a little gem whose interior memorials, three-decker pulpit and heraldic glass contrast nicely with its simple exterior'. St Mary's is Saxon in origin, with typical high narrow proportions. Other than its general design, a group of megalith quoin stones at the west end, and the pilasters on the north nave wall, are evidence of these Saxon origins. In years past, two of Oxford University's great public orators were rectors at St Mary's. William Crowe, a poet and divine, was the incumbent between 1787 and 1829, and was followed by Augustus W Hare, a writer and preacher. With such a beautiful setting, looking across open countryside to the imposing chalk downs, it is no surprise to find that the village was able to attract men of such calibre.

Honeystreet is a community that owes its origins entirely to the coming of the canal. The Barge Inn was a 'service station' of its day, purveying not just ales and stout to the thirsty bargees, but also acting as a brewery, a bakery, and a slaughterhouse. Late 19th century photographs of the Barge bear more of a resemblance to a large village store than a mere ale-house! Such was the importance of the inn to passing traffic, that following its destruction by fire in 1858, it was rebuilt in just six months. To the east of the Barge lies the site of Honeystreet Wharf. This was used until the 1940s by Messrs Robbins, Lane and Pinnegar, the last commercial traders to operate the canal between Hungerford and Avonmouth. Their 60 ton barge *Unity* would bring various cargoes to the depths of Wiltshire, including softwood, round timber and phosphates. The phosphates were used to manufacture chemical fertilisers for local farmers, whilst the timber was used in the construction of canal vessels. Many of the narrow boats that operated on the K & A, the Wey Navigation and the Basingstoke Canal were built at Honeystreet. The wharf area today is private property, although an isolated chimney shaft stands as testimony to a former era. A carved stone on the east face of the shaft provides a history of the early years of the canal at Honeystreet:

'K & A Canal finished 1810. This wharf commenced 1811. K & A Road made 1842. Part of Wharf burnt 1854. Rebuilt and enlarged 1855. This chimney erected 1859.'

Honeystreet is a place for such engravings. A more human tale is etched onto a pane of glass at the Barge Inn. The legend reads quite simply: 'Syd Biggs got drunk, May 2nd, 1872'!

Wootton Rivers and Savernake Forest

Introduction: Heading eastwards from the Vale of Pewsey, the Kennet & Avon Canal skirts the southern fringes of Savernake Forest as it finds its summit level. The canal is now over 450 ft above sea-level, compared with a mere 65 ft just 40 miles back in the City of Bath. At its summit, the K & A plunges into Bruce Tunnel, the longest such construction on the whole waterway. This circuit commences at Wootton Rivers, where the canal is followed through a gentle run of four locks to the actual summit pound. Beyond the locks, the K & A passes Burbage Wharf before heading through a deep cutting to reach Bruce Tunnel. This is where we leave the canal to return to Wootton Rivers by way of Savernake Forest, once a royal hunting ground that is still home to several herds of roe and fallow deer.

Distance: A relatively substantial circuit of some 8 miles, where the landscape is undulating rather than hilly. Maps: The majority of the walk lies on the following maps: OS Landranger 174 'Newbury and Wantage', OS Pathfinder SU 26/36 'Hungerford and Savernake Forest'. A small section of the circuit creeps onto Landranger sheet 173 'Swindon and Devizes' and Pathfinder sheet 1185 'Devizes and Marlborough'.

Refreshments: At the end of the walk, the Royal Oak Free House in Wootton Rivers serves all manner of snacks and meals. Alongside Bruce Tunnel is the Savernake Forest Hotel, which opens its doors to non-residents.

How to get there: Leave the A345 Marlborough to Salisbury road at Clench Common, 3 miles south of Marlborough. An unclassified road heads in a south-easterly direction to Wootton Rivers. In the centre

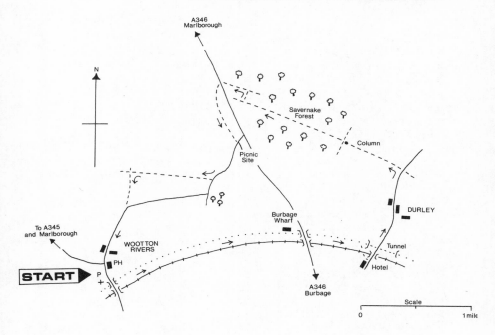

of the village, there is a public carpark alongside the Village Hall. (GR 197 631)

The Walk: Leave the carpark, turn right and follow the road through the village to the point where it crosses the K & A canal. Just before the canal bridge, a path on the right leads to St Andrew's church. Head to the east (left) along the towpath for 2½ miles until you reach the western portal of Bruce Tunnel. This section of towpath includes locks 51 to 54, the Wootton Rivers flight, as well as Burbage Wharf with its replica crane. The final approach to Bruce Tunnel is through a finely wooded cutting.

Alongside the tunnel, follow the steps on the right to reach a path that passes beneath the main West of England Railway. Continue along this path to reach the road alongside the Savernake Forest Hotel. It is worth crossing this road and making a detour along the footpath opposite that leads to the eastern entrance to the tunnel. The entrance is just 300 yards from the road.

Follow the road northwards from the hotel for ¾ mile to the far side of the hamlet of Durley. Just beyond this settlement, a fine prospect awaits you. To the right, a grand driveway leads up to the frontage of Tottenham House, whilst to the left a wide grassy ride stretches away to the Ailesbury Monument.

Follow this ride towards the impressive monument, beyond which you cross a forest road and follow a woodland path through Savernake Forest, all the while keeping in the same north-easterly direction.

In almost one mile, you will hear the sound of traffic on the A346 Marlborough road just 100 yards ahead. At this point, turn right onto a side track, then left at the gravelled track you reach in just 150 yards. Follow this track through to the main road. Cross *with care*, and follow a path opposite that continues beyond a single-bar wooden fence. This path bears to the left and borders the western edge of Savernake Forest for ½ mile before joining a quiet lane that leads to Wootton Rivers.

Turn right, avoiding the tempting left turn into a picnic site, and follow the Wootton road for ½ mile. It eventually descends via a series of bends to pass beneath the bridge abutments of the old Marlborough railway. Almost immediately after the abutments, turn right onto a bridlepath, named 'Mud Lane' on the OS Pathfinder sheet. You have been warned! This delightful green lane heads westwards across the hilltop, with fine views over Wootton Rivers to the hills beyond. In ¾ mile, turn left at an obvious junction, and follow another bridlepath downhill for ½ mile to join the Wootton road.

Turn right, and almost immediately you are back in Wootton Rivers. Continue along the village street, past the Royal Oak, until you reach the Village Hall and your vehicle.

Historical Notes

Wootton Rivers is essentially a linear settlement, with the brick cottages and thatched dwellings, the church and the chapel, the village hall and the pub, all arrayed along a one mile section of the village's main street. St Andrew's church lies alongside the southern end of this main street, and is constructed of flint and grey blue sarsen, together with a dressing of limestone. Local guidebooks all make note of the unique church clock, built in 1911 to commemorate the Coronation of George V. Jack Spratt, its architect, collected various materials ranging from chaff cutters and pipes, to reaping machines and bedsteads, to use in its construction. The face is adorned with letters rather than numbers, and the clock chimes out a different tune every ¼ hour over a six-hour cycle. Another odd tale in the history of Wootton Rivers relates to its long defunct railway halt on the London to the West of England mainline. Being unmanned, passengers were obliged to purchase their tickets at the nearby Royal Oak public house – quite an acceptable waiting-room in which to sit out a two-hour delay!

The Wootton Rivers Locks: The Long Pound extends for 15 miles from Devizes through to Wootton Rivers, where the canal makes its final push for the summit. The Wootton Rivers flight of four locks – Wootton Rivers, Heathy Close, Brimslade and Cadley – raise the canal some 35 ft to its summit level above Cadley, which then runs for just 2½ miles eastwards to Crofton Top Lock. The four locks were abandoned in a state of sad disrepair in the 1950s, but by 1973 had become the first locks to be renovated and reopened along the whole of the Wiltshire section of the canal. St John's College in Cambridge owned substantial landholdings in the Wootton Rivers area, and insisted that 'carriage bridges' be created across the K & A. Not only had there to be enough width to accommodate a horse and carriage, there also had to be the minimum of incline on the bridge approaches. This explains the absence of the humpback bridge around Wootton Rivers, an ever so common sight on the rest of Britain's canal network.

Burbage Wharf was constructed at the behest of the Earl of Ailesbury, the local landowner, in the early 19th century. The building materials used in its construction were a mixture of imported Bath stone and local bricks, each brick marked with a letter 'A' to denote Ailesbury's ownership of the wharf. The wharf was the nearest point that the canal came to Marlborough, and a steady trade built up in timber, coal, stone and agricultural produce. A splendid crane was erected at Burbage to handle these cargoes. Its centre post, 2 ft in diameter, supported a jib some 20 ft in length. To stabilise such a construction, 2 tons of stone blocks were used as ballast. By 1971, the original crane had to be demolished with its ruinous state presenting a safety hazard. A team of industrial archaeologists, keen to reconstruct a replica of the crane on site, drew up detailed plans of its structure and dimensions. The Crown Estates offered a supply of timber, and a group of soldiers from the REME workshops at Tidworth recreated the Burbage Crane!

The Bruce Tunnel, with its 502 ft length and 17 ft width, is second only to the Netherton Tunnel, on the Birmingham Canal Navigation, in terms of cross-sectional dimensions on Britain's navigable waterways. The need for a tunnel is perhaps questionable, given that deep cuttings were excavated at either approach to the tunnel which then proceeds to pierce what is nothing more than a low hillock. The answer lies in the fact that the Earl of Ailesbury insisted that the tunnel was constructed in order to minimise the visual impact that the waterway made upon his estate. There was no towpath through the Bruce Tunnel, the bargees hauling themselves through its length by means of a chain fastened to the brickwork of the south wall, whilst the horses were unfastened and led across the hilltop. The bricks, you may recall, came from the brickworks alongside Caen Hill at Devizes (Walk 7). The western portal of the tunnel carries a blank plaque, whilst the eastern portal is inscribed with a detail recording the origins of the name 'Bruce':

'The Kennet and Avon Canal Company inscribe this tunnel with the name Bruce in testimony of their gratitude for the uniform and effectual support of the Right Honourable Thomas Bruce, Earl of Ailesbury, and Charles, Lord Bruce, his son, through the whole progress of this national work by which a direct communication by water was opened between the cities of London and Bristol. Anno Domini 1810.'

Incidentally, both Burbage Wharf and the Bruce Tunnel stand on the canal's summit, which runs for some 2½ miles just above the 450 ft contour. This is one of the shortest summit levels on the inland waterway network and, from hereon in, it is downhill to Reading and the Thames!

Tottenham House was the ancestral home of the Ailesbury family. The Ailesburys were the great landowners in this part of Wiltshire, and were rightly concerned at the impact that the K & A could have had around their estate. The 1796 Canal Act actually stipulated that the engines at Crofton Pumping Station should 'consume their own smoke' to avoid disturbing the landed gentry down the road! Enginemen failing to observe this regulation were liable to dismissal from the K & A Canal Company. The Ailesburys, however, did benefit from the construction of the canal's reservoir at Wilton, with Tottenham House obtaining its first regular pumped water supply from Wilton Water. Running for almost two miles to the west of Tottenham House is the Column Ride, which culminates at the most impressive Ailesbury Monument (see below). At the end of the day, however, the Ailesburys must have welcomed the arrival of the K & A, for a plaque at the eastern end of the Bruce Tunnel (see above) records the K & A Canal Company's gratitude for their 'uniform and effectual support'. On balance, the guarantee of domestic water supplies at Tottenham House, combined with a wharf on the estate at Burbage, probably outweighed the drawbacks of the occasional drunk bargee and his accompanying crew.

Savernake Forest extends for over 2,300 acres across an undulating plateau high above Marlborough. Prior to the Conquest, the forest embraced a much larger slice of the Wiltshire countryside, and was a noted royal hunting ground. To this day, herds of roe and fallow deer still roam the deeper parts of Savernake. From the centre of the forest, eight fine avenues of beech trees radiate outwards, following a design attributed to Capability Brown. In the south-eastern corner of the forest lies the Ailesbury Monument, a Classical construction erected by Thomas Bruce, Earl of Ailesbury. The plaques that adorn the memorial record three reasons for its construction – it stands in memory of Charles Bruce, a former Earl of Ailesbury, who left the estates hereabouts to his nephew Thomas; it speaks of Thomas' gratitude to George III for his conferral of an Earldom; and it records thanks to Almighty God for releasing George III from a prolonged and miserable illness. This last claim gives substance to the view that the monument was erected primarily to commemorate George III's recovery from madness!

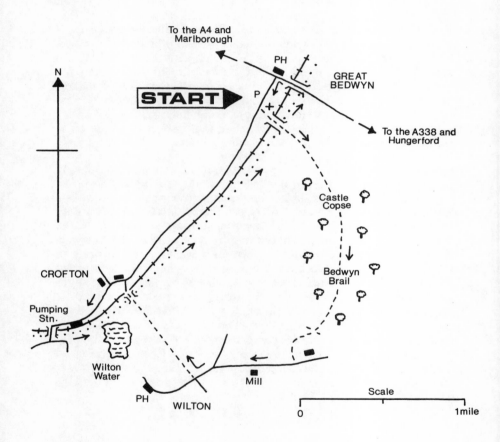

N

To the A4 and
Marlborough

PH

GREAT
BEDWYN

START

P

To the A338 and
Hungerford

Castle
Copse

CROFTON

Bedwyn
Brail

Pumping
Stn.

Wilton
Water

Mill

PH

WILTON

Scale

0   1mile

Crofton and Great Bedwyn

Introduction: Crofton and Great Bedwyn lie just to the east of the Kennet & Avon Canal's summit pound. From now on, it is a steady descent to the Thames at Reading. At the summit level of any waterway, a reliable water supply is an absolute necessity. Literally hundreds of thousands of gallons of the precious liquid will be flowing out through the locks in both directions. The K & A's supply comes from Wilton Water, an artificial lake, where steam engines at the nearby Crofton Pumping Station were originally used to raise the water to the actual summit level. This undulating circuit explores the fascinating canalside environment in and around Crofton and Great Bedwyn, as well as taking in a fine stretch of countryside to the south-east of the canal. This includes Bedwyn Brail, an extensive area of mixed woodland; Wilton Windmill, high on its lonely hillside; and a fine stretch of unmetalled Roman road crossing the hilltop between Wilton and Crofton. Undeniably, a five-star excursion!

Distance: A 7 mile circuit that includes just the occasional gentle climb. Maps: OS Landranger sheet 174 'Newbury and Wantage'; OS Pathfinder sheet SU 26/36 'Hungerford and Savernake Forest'.

Refreshments: At the end of the walk, there are two public houses in Great Bedwyn – the Cross Keys and the Three Tuns. The Swan Inn at Wilton lies just minutes off the actual route (see map).

How to get there: Five miles east of Marlborough on the A4, a minor road turns off in a southerly direction towards Great Bedwyn. In the village, turn right into Church Street, and park on the roadside near the church (GR 277 643)

The Walk: Continue along Church Street in Great Bedwyn until, just past St Mary's church, you turn left to follow a footpath signposted to 'Bedwyn Brail'. The path borders the churchyard before crossing the main West of England Railway and the K & A Canal. Cross the stile immediately ahead of you, bear to the right for 20 yards and then climb the slope to the stile on the left-hand side. Beyond this stile, follow the right-hand hedgerow across several fields until you reach Castle Copse. It is worth pausing along this fieldpath to enjoy the views back across Great Bedwyn. In the corner of the last field, you will find a stile that gives access to the woodland. A clear warning sign tells walkers to adhere to the public footpaths!

Follow the main distinct path through the trees until you reach a large clearing. Continue across this clearing, keeping approximately 20 yards to the left of its right-hand boundary, until you see a metalled forestry track ahead. This track is then followed for one mile southwards through the woodland, where various enclosures provide clues to the function of this wood – the rearing of young pheasants! The woodland track ends at a gate, with a cottage 150 yards ahead.

Turn right beyond the gate to follow a bridlepath around the edge of the open field on your left-hand side. You will emerge onto a lane where the road is followed to the right through to Wilton, via the village windmill. On the very edge of Wilton, follow the bridlepath signposted on the right-hand side as leading to the Crofton Beam Engines. There is also a road to the left at this point leading to Marten. The bridlepath is in fact an old Roman road, unmetalled and unincorporated into the modern road network. Wilton Water (of which more later) is tucked away in the valley to the left whilst beyond, a quite respectable view opens up of the Wiltshire countryside. The Roman road drops to cross the K & A and the railway, and shortly you reach a road junction.

Turn left and follow the road for ½ mile through Crofton to the K & A at Freewarren Bridge. En route you will pass Crofton Pumping Station, as well as crossing the canal feeder channel that carries water from Wilton Water to the canal's summit level.

Follow the towpath to the left back to Great Bedwyn Wharf, where you leave the canal and follow the road to the left back into Bedwyn village where the walk began. The features along the towpath include Wilton Water, half a dozen locks and a millstream that runs parallel to the K & A between Mill Bridge and Bedwyn Church Lock. The mill is no more, but water still flows from the canal into the stream.

Historical Notes

Great Bedwyn was actually a market town with borough status from the 11th century through to the Reform Act of 1832, and at one time returned two Members of Parliament – not bad for a settlement of just 1,060 people! The village has a long tradition of stone masonry, associated with the Lloyd family whose premises are located in Church Street. The Lloyds originally came to the area from the Midlands to work on the K & A, one Benjamin Lloyd being employed on the construction of the Bruce Tunnel in 1803. Benjamin Lloyd was later employed as 'agent for the superintendence of masonry'. The Church Street premises are open to the public as a Stone Museum and contain many examples of the stone-mason's art. These include restored and painted texts, fonts, statuary and mounted fossils. Almost opposite the museum lies St Mary the Virgin church. The dominant internal feature is the 12th century nave, where circular pillars support handsomely carved arches. The church monuments include an effigy of Sir John Seymour, whose daughter married Henry VIII in 1536, and a number of windows within the north transept dedicated to the Ailesbury family (see Walk 10). Great Bedwyn Wharf, where we take leave of the K & A, used to boast two coal merchants. This is yet another reminder of the importance of the coal trade to the canal's early fortunes. The K & A Canal owed a great deal to those seemingly insignificant few miles of Coal Canal that ran from Dundas to Paulton and the North Somerset collieries. Commerce is still carried on at the Wharf today, only now it is in the form of boat repairs.

Wilton Windmill, a five-storey brick tower mill, was built in 1821. The mill was fully operational until the 1890s, when a period of gentle decay and dereliction set in. By the 1920s, the mill was officially closed down and its various mechanical parts removed. Between 1971 and 1976, under the sponsorship of the Wiltshire Historic Buildings Trust, Wilton Windmill was lovingly restored to full working order. It stands proudly on the hillside between Wilton and Shalbourne as Wiltshire's only complete surviving mill. Its technical details include a domed cap, two common sails and two patent sails. During most Sunday afternoons in the summer months the mill is fully operational, enabling visitors to see local corn being ground into flour. Prospective visitors should telephone 0672-870268 for full details.

Roman road: Between the mill and Crofton, the walk follows a fine section of Roman road that has fortunately escaped the Highways Department and their tarmacadam. This is thought to be a section of the routeway that linked Cunetio (Mildenhall near Marlborough) with Venta Belgarum (Winchester). Fine views open up as the road crosses the crest of the hill, although Wilton Water is disappointingly hidden out of sight in the valley below. Also out of eye-shot is the spire of Salisbury Cathedral although local rumour has suggested that this 404 ft pinnacle can be seen from the hilltop!

Crofton Pumping Station: The 1794 Kennet & Avon Canal Act had envisaged a lower summit level for the canal than that actually constructed. This lower level would have included a 4,312 yard tunnel along its 18 mile pound. The expense of such a project led to today's higher level summit being cut, which in turn necessitated a pumping station to replenish the loss of water supplies down through the lock chambers. A pair of Cornish beam engines were installed in the pump house at Crofton, an 1812 Boulton and Watt together with an 1845 Harvey's of Hayle. Both have been carefully restored and returned to full working order, and are believed to be the oldest operational steam engines in the world. Alongside the pumping station lies Wilton Water, an eight acre reservoir formed by the damming of a spring-fed stream that trickles down the valley from nearby Wilton village. Water is lifted a height of 40 ft from Wilton Water to the canal's summit by way of Crofton Leat, a small channel that runs westwards for almost a mile from the pumping station to Crofton Top Lock and the summit pound. Today's pumping operations are carried out by electric pumps, although the restored beam engines are in steam on occasional summer weekends (telephone 0491-874072 for details). Somewhat appropriately, it was Sir John Betjeman who reopened Crofton Pumping Station in 1970, following its restoration. If steam and pumps and machinery are not your forte, then Wilton Water will inevitably attract your eye. This is a birdwatcher's paradise, where common species such as the mallard and the tufted duck occasionally paddle alongside both pochard and teal, far less common species of wildfowl.

Little Bedwyn and Hungerford

Introduction: East of Crofton, the Kennet & Avon Canal begins its gradual descent towards Berkshire, Reading and the Thames. As our footsteps pass between Little Bedwyn and Hungerford, almost imperceptibly we pass from Wiltshire across the border into the Royal County of Berkshire. There are no fanfares as the Kennet Valley approaches. As an early reminder of the clear chalk stream that lies ahead, this particular walk follows a tributary valley that carries the sparkling waters of the Dun. It is all a far cry from the brown murky waters of the Avon further west. The circuit explores the border country west of Hungerford, where open pasture and arable land rise on either side of the Dun's valley. The outward leg of the walk follows the hilltops between Hungerford and Little Bedwyn, whilst the return is along the canal's towpath at the foot of the valley. A pleasant – rather than spectacular – pastoral excursion.

Distance: An undulating 7 mile circuit, which includes a lengthy section of road walking albeit along a quiet rural byway. Maps: OS Landranger 174 'Newbury, Wantage and surrounding area' and Pathfinder SU 26/36 'Hungerford and Savernake Forest'.

Refreshments: Hungerford boasts numerous hostelries, whilst in Little Bedwyn the walk passes within yards of the Harrow Inn.

How to get there: Leave the A4 at Hungerford and follow the A338 Salisbury road for ¼ mile into the town centre. Just beyond the railway bridge, turn right into Church Street and park in the public carpark alongside the library (fee payable). (GR 337 685)

The Walk: Leave the carpark and turn right along Church Street, heading away from Hungerford town centre. The next ½ mile sees the walk passing through various housing developments, both ancient

67

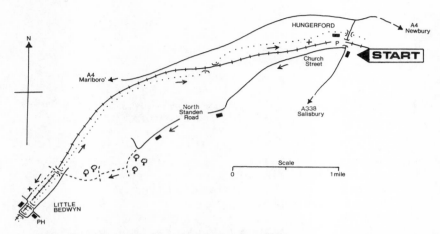

and modern, until the road climbs out of the town and into open countryside just beyond some industrial premises. Although it is road walking for the next couple of miles, it is all rather pleasant. There are no hedgerows or fences, just open views in all directions. Away to the south lie the downs above Inkpen and Shalbourne, whilst just to the north lies the Dun Valley, carrying not only a tributary stream of the Kennet, but also the A4, the K & A and the main West of England railway. This section of road is one of the few places where I have seen signs bearing the legend 'Pheasants – drive with care'! These game birds are a common sight hereabouts, especially at the occasional roadside copse.

Continue along this open country road – labelled as North Standen Road on the OS Pathfinder Map – until 1½ miles out of Hungerford you pass North Standen House on the left-hand side. The 'trades-man's entrance' is a reminder that all is not lost as far as class divisions are concerned in 1990s Britain! A short distance on from North Standen House, a fine iron boundary post on the right marks the Berkshire/Wiltshire border. Below in the valley sits the village of Froxfield, with Somerset Hospital – a group of red brick almshouses – being especially prominent.

A little over ¼ mile on from the boundary, the road bears sharply to the right whilst your route lies directly ahead along a track signposted 'By Way'. Follow this byway for ¼ mile, as it borders Stype Wood, ignoring a tempting left turn into the woodland itself. Turn right at the first opportunity to follow an enclosed path downhill to the south-east corner of Juggs Wood. Cross a cross-track and continue straight ahead along the edge of the woodland. In 100 yards, fork left where the path divides and continue downhill to the Little Bedwyn to Froxfield road.

Cross straight over and follow the gravelled access road opposite across the K & A Canal and the railway line. Having crossed the tracks, turn immediately to the left and follow the field-path that borders the line. At the far left-hand corner of the first field, cross the stile into the paddock beyond. On the opposite side of the paddock is a second stile, beyond which you follow the boundary fence surrounding Little Bedwyn church out onto Church Street.

Having explored this thankfully unlocked building, continue along Church Street, and turn left at the next junction to follow the road through the western side of Little Bedwyn village. Continue along the road as it bears left to cross the K & A, before passing through the opposite side of the village. At the next 'junction' it is right to the Harrow Inn and left to join the K & A towpath. If this sounds rather complicated, don't worry because it is all patently obvious when you are on location!

Turn right on joining the towpath, and follow the canal for 3 miles back into Hungerford. There are eight locks on this section of the K & A, starting with number 67 'Little Bedwyn' and ending with number 74 'Hungerford'. Just beyond number 70 'Froxfield Bottom' is the site of Froxfield Wharf, where the road bridge marks the Berkshire border; the Dun Aqueduct lies just before number 72 'Cobblers Lock'; whilst Hungerford Marsh Lock – number 73 – is almost unique insofar as a swingbridge crosses the lock chamber.

The towpath passes St Lawrence's church in Hungerford before reaching Hungerford Wharf, Hungerford Lock and the Town Bridge. Leave the canal at the Town Bridge and you will find yourself in the High Street. Turn right, pass underneath the railway and Church Street is the first turning on the right.

Historical Notes

Hungerford's history has always been tied in with the various means of communication that pass through the town. Being located on the Bath Road, Hungerford was for many years involved in the coaching trade between London and the West Country. The 19th century saw the K & A Canal arrive in the town, to be shortly superseded by the main West of England railway line. This century in turn has seen the arrival of the M4 motorway in the district, opening up the area to modern commercial development.

The Bear Inn on the London Road is a reminder of the town's great coaching traditions. Although the present buildings date from Georgian times, there has been a hostelry on the site since 1297. Over the years, many illustrious visitors have stopped overnight at the Bear. These have included Queen Elizabeth I and King Charles I, who used the hotel as his headquarters during various skirmishes in the Newbury area in 1643. Samuel Pepys dined at the Bear on 10th June 1688, whilst December of the same year saw its hospitality extend to William of Orange. He actually held court to various envoys in his bedroom at the Bear, and the result of their deliberations was the eventual flight of James II to France, and the end of the House of Stuart. Coaching may seem romantic to today's generation, although in reality it was a tough way of travelling around the country. An 18th century poem entitled *A journey to Bath and Bristol* (Anon) described the route through 'marshy Hungerford that's famed for beer' thus:

'From Hungerford we swift went o'er the Plain,
Too soon we came to the destructive Lane,
O fatal way! Here Rocks and craggy Stones
Our Limbs distorted, and unlock't our Bones,
The long worn Axle to the Coach, alack!
Gave here a dismal, unexpected crack.'

St Lawrence's church in Hungerford is a rebuilding of 1816, in the Gothic style. The former building, still a common sight on old prints, finally collapsed under the weight of heavy snowfall in 1814! The arrival of the K & A Canal in the town meant that Bath stone began to appear as a building material.

Little Bedwyn receives but scanty coverage in local topographical guides, authors focusing instead on its larger neighbour a mile or two to the south-west. Little Bedwyn is literally bisected by the K & A Canal and the main West of England Railway. The western side of the village consists of former Victorian estate housing, leading up to St Michael's church. Norman in origin, its predominant feature is a magnificent stone spire, rising from a diagonally buttressed flint tower. Pevsner was far from flattering in his comments on St

70

Michael's. The east window glass was quite simply described as 'terrible'. Two bridges cross the K & A and the railway, linking the two parts of the village. The road bridge is the higher, trough-like in construction, whilst the lower footbridge would have been a swing-bridge before the arrival of the railway. The eastern half of Little Bedwyn is the older farming community. Especially prominent is the pedimented Georgian Manor Farmhouse. Opposite this fine building lies an unusual octagonal game larder, with an octagonal tiled roof that sweeps up to a weathervane formed into a gilded hog's head!

The K & A Canal between Little Bedwyn and Hungerford contains much of interest. Just to the east of lock 70 'Froxfield Bottom' lies the site of **Froxfield Wharf**. Alongside the wharf, the Froxfield Feeder enters the canal by means of a unique circular weir. The construction is such that only one third of the water supply enters the canal, the remainder being culverted beneath the waterway to continue along a stream that powered the now demolished Oakhill Mill. Froxfield Bridge marks the Wiltshire/Berkshire boundary, and a short detour at this point will bring you into Froxfield village itself. The village's most noted landmark is the Duke of Somerset's Hospital, a group of red-brick almshouses built around a quadrangle and a pinnacled chapel. Back on the canal, the **Dun Aqueduct** lies just to the west of lock number 72 'Cobbler's Lock'. It is worth scrambling down the embankment to view this small brick construction, whose diminutive three arches stand in complete contrast to the majestic curves of Dundas and Avoncliff at the western end of the waterway. Just to the west of Hungerford, the canal borders **Freeman's Marsh**, a jealously guarded piece of common land whose origins date back to John of Gaunt. Although the Marsh Lock severed a right-of-way, this proved no problem to the commoners – a swingbridge was simply erected right across the middle of the lock chamber! This is thought to be a unique sight on the British waterways network. **Hungerford Wharf** first saw commercial traffic in 1798, with the arrival of a barge laden with Russian tallow. The longest occupants of the wharf site were J Woolridge & Son, a firm of local builders, who were awarded the maintenance contract on the eastern end of the K & A Canal between 1851 and 1863. The Woolridges received £3,000 per annum from the canal's then owners, the GWR, in return for keeping the navigation functional between Wootton Rivers and Reading. After an occupancy lasting over 100 years, the firm finally vacated Hungerford Wharf in 1962.

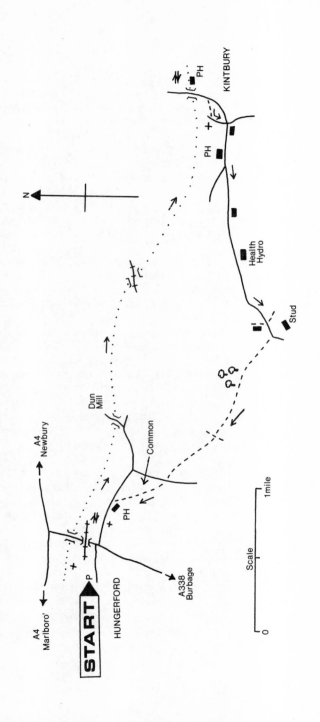

Hungerford and Kintbury

Introduction: Beyond Hungerford, our footsteps are firmly entrenched in the Royal County of Berkshire. After a journey of some 80 miles from the City Docks in Bristol, the river Kennet at last makes its first appearance upon the landscape. Dun Mill marks the confluence of the Dun with the Kennet, whose water meadows then proceed to parallel the Kennet & Avon Canal through to Kintbury. This watery paradise forms the outward leg of our journey. The section of the walk that returns us to Hungerford explores the undulating countryside to the south of the canal. As well as the picturesque village of Kintbury, our explorations include what one guidebook has described as the 'most interesting approach to Hungerford' – the approach from the south across Hungerford Common. Certainly, this fine expanse of open land brings with it extensive views across the town and the neighbouring section of the Kennet Valley. With a selection of locks, Kintbury Wharf, a canalside inn and a number of landed estates, this is a walk that is never short of interest.

Distance: An undulating 7 mile circuit, with nothing more than the most gentle of climbs to negotiate. Maps: OS Landranger 174 'Newbury, Wantage and surrounding area' and Pathfinder SU 26/36 'Hungerford and Savernake Forest'.

Refreshments: There are several hostelries in Kintbury, including the Dundas Arms Hotel alongside the K & A. On the 'town' side of Hungerford Common, the Down Gate public house serves a nourishing plateful of food.

How to get there: Leave the A4 at Hungerford and follow the A338 Salisbury road for ¼ mile into the town centre. Just beyond the railway bridge, turn right into Church Street and park in the public carpark alongside the library (fee payable). (GR 337 685)

The Walk: From the carpark, return to Church Street and turn left to walk the few yards to Hungerford's High Street. Turn left, pass under the railway bridge and continue along the High Street to the K & A Canal. Join the towpath and follow the waterway eastwards (ie. to the right) for the 3 miles to Kintbury. Initially the path follows the south bank of the canal, changing to the north bank at the bridge alongside Dunmill Lock.

Before continuing eastwards at this point, it is worth taking a short detour along the lane to the north. This will bring you to Dun Mill, where a fine group of buildings lie alongside the confluence of the Dun and the Kennet.

Having returned to the canal, continue along the towpath, initially with the river Kennet to your left and the K & A to your right. This watery environment is soon followed by lock 76 'Wire Lock' and lock 77 'Brunsden's Lock'. Crossing the canal between these two points is the main Plymouth and West of England Railway. Coming into Kintbury, St Mary's church is the first landmark, quickly followed by Kintbury Lock and the road into the village.

Turn right at the road, perhaps pausing for refreshment at the canalside Dundas Arms. You will shortly pass Kintbury Mill on your right and, in another 50 yards, look out for a turning on the right signposted 'Private Road leading to the Cliffs'. Follow this turning, which soon becomes a footpath, through to the village church. Having hunted out the Charles Dundas memorial within St Mary's, leave the churchyard by the gate alongside the war memorial, and continue along Church Street to its junction with the High Street.

Turn right, and follow the High Street for 600 yards, passing the Blue Ball Inn, to a fork on the edge of the village. Bear left, a sign indicating that the lane leads to 'Inglewood Health Hydro'. Just over one mile of road walking follows, with the quiet lane passing Kintbury Farm, the Health Hydro, and Templeton Nursery, before it reaches a bridleway on the right-hand side that heads off in front of some estate houses. On the left is the driveway leading to Templeton Stud.

Ignore the bridleway, instead continue along the lane for another 100 yards. The road bears to the left, but your route lies across the gateway on the right-hand side where a public footpath sign points out across an open field. Head straight across the field towards the nearest corner of the wood ahead. Follow the enclosed path alongside the edge of the trees.

Where the woodland ends, ignore this enclosed path as it turns to the right to follow the far side of the copse. Instead, continue ahead in the same general direction, keeping the hedgerow to your right. In 600 yards, you will cross a gravel track that leads to Pink Dairy Farm, beyond which you continue in the same general direction with the hedge still to your right. In another 600 yards, cross the obvious stile on the right to gain access to Hungerford Common. Continue to follow the hedgerow – this time it is to your left – until you reach the road at Inkpen Gate.

Cross over the tarmac, and bear half-right, aiming for the hospital chapel which is just visible at the far side of the common. You will rejoin the road alongside the Down Gate public house, the last semi-rural hostelry before the hustle and bustle of Hungerford's High Street. Turn left at the road, and follow Park Street past the local hospital and its chapel, down to the High Street. Turn right, and Church Street is the first turning on the left.

Historical Notes

The Kennet & Avon Canal: To the east of Hungerford, the river Kennet begins to make its impact upon the canal. A mile out of the town lies lock number 75 '**Dunmill Lock**' named after the local watermill that lies at the confluence of the Dun and the Kennet. The local mill owners kept a critical eye on the minutiae of the various Navigation Acts, for fear that the waterway would draw upon their water supplies. In this case, there appears to have been no real problem, the K & A actually being of positive benefit in terms of improved transport and distribution for the mill. Between **Brunsden's Lock** (number 77) and Kintbury, extensive cress beds lay to the south of the canal. This delicacy was carried eastwards to Kintbury by punt, from where the railway would transport the cress to the streets of the capital within hours. One can imagine the limp and sorry state that the produce would have been in had the entire journey been by water at little more than 4 mph!

The Kennet reminds us of its presence by actually joining the canal for 200 yards either side of Kintbury church, flowing in beneath the towpath from the north before forking off to the right to power a local mill. The final stretch of towpath on this ramble brings us through to **Kintbury Lock** and the adjoining wharf. Appropriately, the lock was officially reopened on the 3rd December 1972 by a Miss W Rennie. If the name sounds familiar, it is because one of Miss

Rennie's distant relatives was a certain John Rennie, the K & A Canal Engineer back in the pioneering days. **Kintbury Wharf** was the scene of much celebration some 175 years earlier when, on the 12th June 1797, the first section of the canal from Newbury to the wharf was officially opened. A 60 ton barge arrived from Newbury, conveying the band of the 15th Regiment of Dragoons, the six mile journey being completed in 2½ hours. Charles Dundas, the K & A Canal Company Chairman, and his committee, greeted the party, and the rest, as they say, is history. Trade at the wharf flourished. Iron and coke would arrive from South Wales for the local forges, where agricultural equipment was manufactured, whilst westwards to Bristol would go the whiting ground from the local chalk. Incidentally, the Dragoons took an extra hour to return to Newbury, which might have had not a little to do with the hospitality shown at the local inn, now appropriately named the Dundas Arms.

Kintbury is an attractive village of brick-and-tile cottages located in the Kennet Valley. The river lends its name to the settlement, which can be literally translated 'Kennet borough'. Historically, Kintbury has always been an agricultural community, although there have been sporadic industrial developments that have included whiting production, brick and tile manufacture and silk weaving. The village's economic dependence upon the land is vividly illustrated by a series of events that occurred in 1830. Local farm labourers, concerned at the mechanisation of their livelihood, had been engaged in periodic bouts of rioting, rick burning and actual destruction of farm machinery. A veritable group of rural Luddites! The local Yeomanry, led by Lords Craven and Dundas, were unable to restore law and order within the community, with the result that a detachment of Grenadier Guards was summoned from the capital. The rebellion was quelled as a result of a raid on the Blue Ball Inn, the rioters' headquarters, and over 100 men were arrested. One was subsequently executed at Reading, whilst the others were either transported or imprisoned.

The local Manor of Kintbury Amesbury passed into the hands of the aforementioned Dundas family in 1790. Charles Dundas was the first Chairman of the Kennet and Avon Canal Company, an achievement which is recorded on a monument in St Mary's church, Kintbury. Dundas was a great public servant, representing Berkshire in Parliament for over 50 years. He was later to become Baron Amesbury, a title he held until his death from cholera in 1832. These facts are inscribed within St Mary's, whose 12th century origins have been largely lost as a result of much Victorian 'improvement'.

Less factual is the legend of the Kintbury Great Bell, which was cast into the river Kennet when a terrific storm destroyed the church tower some time during the dark ages of ecclesiastical history. Following a wizard's strict commands, a chain pulled by twelve white heifers was used in an attempt to rescue the bell. This merry procession was led by twelve maidens arrayed in white with red sashes. The whole operation was to be carried out in strict silence – just one spoken word would destroy the chain. The Kintbury witch, however, was to have none of this. She suddenly appeared and exclaimed:

'Here comes the great Kintbury bell
In spite of all the devils in hell.'

The spell was broken, the chain was destroyed and the bell returned to its watery grave.

Hungerford Common, together with Freeman's Marsh, are areas of common grazing and fishing rights that were bestowed upon the local townsfolk back in the 14th century by John of Gaunt. To this day, a Hocktide Court is the jealous custodian of these common rights. At 8 am each Easter Tuesday, the Town Crier announces to the people of Hungerford that the court will be assembling at 9 am. Whilst the rules relating to the fishing and grazing entitlements are being read, two tithingmen – known locally as 'tutti-men' – visit the homes of the Commoners. The man of the house is called upon to pay up the princely sum of one penny, whilst the women and children merely supply a kiss! An accompanying 'orange scrambler' then donates an orange to each household. A civic luncheon is held for the Court officials, who subsequently 'shoe the colt'. This is the process whereby a local blacksmith drives a horse-nail into the sole of the shoe of any strangers in the midst. Upon crying 'punch', the hammering ceases and the stranger has thereby announced to the gathering his willingness to supply the liquid refreshment needed to satisfy the thirsts of the officials. The stranger is then welcomed into the ranks of the Hungerford men. It could only happen in England! (Further notes on Hungerford can be read in Walk 12 'Little Bedwyn and Hungerford.)

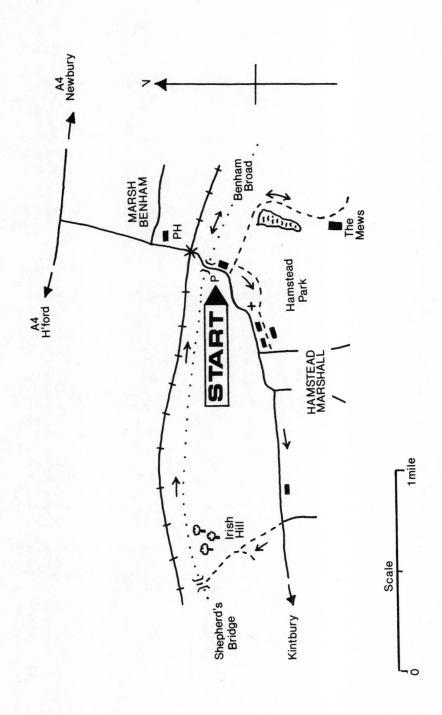

Hamstead Park and Irish Hill

Introduction: As the Kennet & Avon Canal approaches Newbury, the river Kennet begins to make an ever increasing impact upon the landscape. This short circuit, in the vicinity of the village of Hamstead Marshall, is dominated by the Kennet Valley. The river and the canal follow a parallel and at times identical course, whilst in Hamstead Marshall itself the Kennet's waters are diverted via a series of sluices and channels to power a local mill. Away from the canal towpath, the walk explores the edges of Hamstead Park, one of Berkshire's great landed estates, as well as making the gentle ascent of Irish Hill to bring far-ranging views of the neighbourhood. A fine pastoral excursion through an idyllic rural landscape.

NB Two detours are suggested at the end of the walk. One explores Benham Broad, a landscaped section of the K & A designed to smooth its passage through the gentle surroundings of Hamstead Park; whilst the other offers the walker a chance to explore the park itself, with its fishponds and stately mansion.

Distance: A gentle 3½ miles, with the ascent of Irish Hill being a mere 100 ft of climbing! Maps: OS Landranger Sheet 174 'Newbury, Wantage and surrounding area' and OS Pathfinder Sheet SU 46/56 'Newbury' both cover this circuit. The perfectionist, however, will also require OS Pathfinder Sheet SU 26/36 'Hungerford and Savernake Forest' onto which 300 yards of the circuit creep!

Refreshments: In Marsh Benham, ¼ mile north of Hamstead Bridge, the Red House is an attractive thatched inn. On the actual walk there are no refreshment facilities.

79

How to get there: Just 3 miles west of Newbury on the A4 Bath Road, turn left onto a minor road signposted to Hamstead Marshall and Marsh Benham. One mile south of the A4, this road crosses the K & A Canal and the Kennet at Hamstead Bridge. There is room for careful roadside parking at the southern end of the bridge. (GR 423 670)

The Walk: Follow the road southwards from Hamstead Bridge, past Hamstead Mill on your left-hand side, and almost immediately turn left along the access road that leads into Hamstead Park. Turn right just beyond the cattle grid at the entrance to the park and follow a prominent footpath uphill through an avenue of sycamore trees. At the top of the rise, follow the path as it bears to the right to pass through an elegant pair of gateposts, Hamstead church to your right. The field to your left is surrounded by several pairs of similar gateposts, all standing in splendid isolation. These were the entrances to Craven House, which was destroyed during th 19th century.

Continue along a gravelled private road, elegant barn conversions lining your route, until you join a country lane. Turn right, and left at the junction ahead, to follow the Kintbury turning. Continue along the Kintbury road (keeping right at the first junction) for ¾ mile until you reach the second junction, a left-turn signposted Old Lane. En route you will have descended into Peartree Bottom and passed a delightful thatched cottage, Peartree Cottage.

At the junction, look out for a stile in the hedgerow on the right-hand side. Cross this stile, and head half-left across the open field ahead towards a prominent isolated oak tree. Beyond this fine specimen of *Quercus robur*, continue across this hillside field to a stile beneath a second oak tree. You are almost at the top of Irish Hill. Beyond the stile, cross a small paddock to a second stile, some 30 yards distant, where a track is joined.

Continue along this track for 50 yards to a point where it bears left, crosses a cattle grid, and descends the far side of Irish Hill to join the K & A Canal at Shepherd's Bridge. The hillside descent brings with it good views of the Kennet Valley.

Head eastwards (right) along the canal for 2 miles until you reach Hamstead Bridge, just beyond Hamstead Lock. This 2 miles of towpath includes a couple of other locks, Dreweat's and Copse, as well as a short section of waterway that incorporates the river Kennet. Your vehicle should be parked alongside the bridge.

A couple of interesting detours suggest themselves at this point. Continuing along the towpath for just ½ mile brings you to Benham Broad. This is a point where the river Kennet literally crosses the canal to form a wide landscaped section of waterway. This would have formed an aesthetically pleasing feature as the K & A passed along the northern boundary of Hamstead Park.

Another detour involves returning to the entrance to the park and following the driveway across the northern end of the estate fishponds and on to the stately mansion itself – now a nursing home. The round trip to the house is a distance of some 1½ miles.

Historical Notes

Hamstead Marshall, a traditional farming community, was first mentioned in the Domesday Book. Dominating the village and its surroundings is the magnificent 700-acre estate of Hamstead Park. As far back as the 15th century, Richard III was enjoying visits to the shooting lodge in the estate and noting the fine sport in his correspondence. From 1620 through to 1984, the estate was in the hands of the Craven family. William Craven (1606–1697) was knighted by Charles I in 1627, and within the short space of just one week he had become Baron Craven of Hamstead Marshall. During the Civil War he helped to swell the King's coffers, although following the beheading of Charles, public opinion turned against him. Perhaps the politest comment that was passed on the Baron was that he was an 'offender against the Commonwealth of England'. The fine house, originally the home of Earl Marshall, was built by the Dutch entrepreneur, painter and architect Sir Balthazar Gerbier, and was allegedly modelled on Heidelberg Castle. The truth of this claim will have to go undisputed since fire destroyed the property in 1718. All that remains today are the entrance gate posts standing in splendid isolation in the fields to the east of **St Mary's church**, a most evocative sight. The church itself is Norman in origin, with some major 14th century revisions. The interior is particularly atmospheric (if you can penetrate the normally locked doors) being dominated by a fine series of box pews and a three-decker pulpit. Incidentally, the red brick wall that surrounds Hamstead Park is unique insofar as it is thought to be the only 'Listed' wall in England. Sadly, a combination of factors including the need to pay death duties, led to the Craven family vacating the Park in 1984. The property is now listed on the OS maps as a mere 'Nursing Home'.

Whiting: The area around Kintbury and Hamstead Marshall is literally chalk country, with $CaCO_3$ – carbonate of lime – forming the local bedrock. At one time, there were five whiting mills in the Kintbury area. Whiting is a fine powder, produced by extracting soft chalk, soaking it in water and running off the resulting slurry from settling tanks. In its dried powder-like form, it was used in the manufacture of paint. The Berkshire whiting was shipped westwards along the K & A to Bristol's paint manufacturers, a trade that continued until the 1930s. Hidden in Irish Hill Copse, the woodland that lies between Irish Hill and the K & A Canal, are the ruinous remains of one of the local whiting mills.

The K & A Canal between Shepherd's Bridge and Hamstead Lock marks one of the first appearances of the river Kennet as part of the navigation. East of Kintbury, the K & A becomes ever more the canalised river Kennet. Just below Copse Lock, the Kennet enters from the left-hand bank of the canal to form the waterway for just 400 yards, before leaving the canal scene to power Hamstead Mill. If you follow the suggested detour beyond Hamstead Bridge, you will reach Benham Broad, an artificial lake also known as 'The Broads'. This is a section of the canal where the Kennet flows in and out of the navigation forming a wide expanse of water akin to Wilcot Wide Water further west. It was designed to add aesthetic qualities to the waterway as it passed through the estate of the local landed gentry. This landscaping of the K & A might appear strange to today's visitor, but it must be remembered that back in the 18th century, landowners treated the arrival of a canal with the same sort of disdain that today greets a proposed motorway! Incidentally, Hamstead Lock was the first lock to be rebuilt west of Newbury as part of the canal's restoration programme. Back in 1971, upon completion, the work had cost the grand sum of £3,000!

The Great Western Railway was born as a result of a meeting of Bristol merchants way back in 1832. The first section of line was opened between London and Maidenhead on 4th June 1838, and within seven years a through route was being operated from London to Exeter, courtesy of the GWR to Bristol and the Bristol & Exeter Railway to Devon. This route to the west, however, was unceremoniously nicknamed the 'Great Way Round' with its two sections forming two sides of a triangle. The missing third side would have formed a more direct West of England mainline. Ironically, this was finally constructed not as a single engineering project but as a result of the gaps being closed on a patchwork of existing branchlines. Hungerford had its branch line in 1847, coming out from Reading. Further west, a line between Westbury and Yeovil, via Castle Cary, was opened in 1856, six years before the Hungerford line was extended through to Devizes. In 1900, Devizes was linked up with Westbury, and within five years a through route existed with Taunton with the construction of a line from Castle Cary to Langport. It sounds all very complicated, but it essentially meant that Exeter-bound trains could avoid the 'Great Way Round' via Bristol by bearing south-west at Reading and heading out through Newbury, Westbury and Taunton. This is now the main West of England Railway that runs parallel to the K & A between Wootton Rivers and Reading. As you follow the towpath, whether at Bedwyn, Hungerford, Kintbury or Hamstead Marshall, the Inter City 125s will be a familiar sound just a few yards north of the K & A Canal.

Newbury: Between Hamstead Marshall and our next walk at Woolhampton, we are giving the attractive town of Newbury a miss. Mapping out a circular walk in the area is difficult due to various 'obstructions' – Greenham Common Airfield and the local racecourse being but the most obvious. A visit to the town to view the local lock, the Town Bridge and the area around the former wharf is well worth while, however. Equally, a linear excursion from Newbury to either Thatcham or Woolhampton is a possibility, with the local rail service providing the necessary transport back-up. These eastern outskirts of Newbury are dominated by light industrial development, perhaps not the most scenic of environments along the K & A, although at Monkey Marsh (GR 525 662) the local lock was originally turf-sided and makes an interesting feature for visitors. Turf-sided locks were common along the Kennet Navigation, and consisted of turfed sides that sloped away at an angle of 45 degrees from the waterway. This meant wider lock chambers, as can be seen at Monkey Marsh to this day.

83

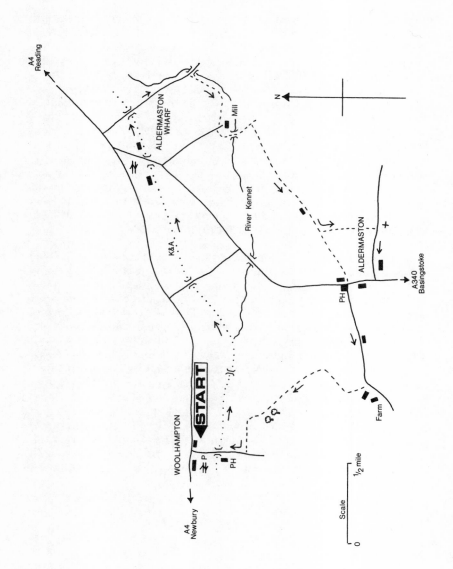

A4
Reading

ALDERMASTON WHARF

Mill

River Kennet

K&A

N

ALDERMASTON

A340
Basingstoke

+

PH

START

WOOLHAMPTON

P

PH

Farm

A4
Newbury

Scale

0

½ mile

Woolhampton and Aldermaston

Introduction: The Kennet Navigation between Newbury and Reading received the Royal Assent in 1715. This mixture of artificial cut and navigable river was finally completed some nine years later under the watchful eye of its chief engineer, John Hore. Walk 15 explores a section of the Navigation running between Woolhampton, Aldermaston Wharf and Padworth Bridge, that includes a fine one mile 'river' section of the waterway. Aldermaston was, of course, the focus of annual 'Ban the Bomb' marches in the 1950s and 1960s. Despite these associations with atomic research, however, the village is remarkably attractive. A most pleasant and restful rural excursion, that contrasts sharply with the final ramble, the hustle and bustle of Reading and the Thames (Walk 16).

Distance: A generally level 6½ mile circuit, that includes one mile of road walking in and around Aldermaston. Maps: The walk extends across Landranger sheets 174 'Newbury and Wantage' and 175 'Reading and Windsor'. Similarly, the walk extends across two Pathfinder sheets – SU 46/56 and SU 66/76.

Refreshments: At the very end of the walk, you will pass the Row Barge Inn alongside the K & A in Woolhampton. In Aldermaston, with 2 miles of walking to go, the circuit passes the 17th century Hind's Head Inn.

How to get there: Woolhampton lies 6 miles east of Newbury on the main A4. Approaching from the west, turn right in the centre of the village to park at the local railway station. The station is actually named 'Midgham' to avoid confusion with 'Wolverhampton'. Evidently, early travellers bound for the Black Country were often to be found stranded in the depths of the Berkshire countryside! (GR 573 667)

The Walk: Leave the station carpark, turn right and follow the lane across the level crossing and southwards to the K & A Canal alongside the Row Barge Inn. Cross the K & A, and follow the towpath eastwards (left) for ½ mile. This section of the waterway is a navigable section of the river Kennet, a fact rather given away by the sinuous route that the fast-flowing river has carved out (most un-canal-like!)

Cross the river at Wickham Knight footbridge, and continue along the towpath on the opposite bank. In less than ½ mile, the Kennet and the K & A divide, the river forking to the right to head off to Aldermaston Mill, whilst your route continues along the towpath to Froudes Bridge. Here the path reverts to the south bank of the canal through to Aldermaston Lock and the adjoining lift-bridge where, once again, you return to the north bank of the K & A for the remaining ½ mile of towpath past Padworth Lock and onto Padworth Bridge.

Cross the canal via the bridge, and continue along the road as it borders the Kennet, Padworth House being a prominent landmark on the hillside ahead. In less than ½ mile, just before the road crosses the river Kennet, follow a footpath on the right-hand side that borders the river. The river bank is followed for ½ mile to a hedgerow – a dead end – where you cross a stile and continue through an area of bush and scrub for just 100 yards to a lane leading to Padworth Mill.

Turn right at the lane and, in just 100 yards, bear left onto a footpath beneath a large horse chestnut tree. This path borders a line of conifers before crossing a series of millstreams by means of various sluices. These sluices guide the waters of the Kennet through to Padworth Mill. Just beyond the final footbridge and sluice, the path crosses a stile into an open field. Head directly across this field to the line of trees ahead, where you cross a small drainage ditch using a plank footbridge. Turn immediately to the right and follow this ditch across two fields until you join a track that ultimately leads through to Aldermaston village.

In ½ mile, this track passes Fisherman's Cottage. In another ¼ mile, turn left onto a signposted footpath that heads uphill across the fields to reach Aldermaston church. At the brow of the hill, just before crossing the stile onto the road, it is worth pausing to enjoy the fine view to the north of this section of the Kennet Valley. Turn right at the road – perhaps having made the detour to explore the normally locked church – and continue for a few hundred yards to the junction with the main A340 alongside an imposing entrance to Aldermaston Court.

Turn right at the main road, and follow the pavement through the village of Aldermaston to the Hind's Head Inn. The many red-brick cottages that line the roadside will inevitably catch your eye. At the mini-roundabout in front of the inn, turn left and follow the road signposted to Brimpton. In ¾ mile, just before Wasing Lower Farm, turn right onto a waymarked path. This is in fact a farm track which is followed to the right of a small airstrip before it emerges into an open field. The path then bears to the left towards a prominent row of trees some 400 yards distant. Follow the path as it passes to the right of the trees. Where the trees end, the path bears to the right, underneath a set of telegraph wires to the edge of the field. Turn left to continue along the same path as it passes a sewage works before joining the Woolhampton road.

Turn right, and in no time at all you will have crossed the K & A Canal and the main railway line to arrive back at Midgham Station carpark – unless the Row Barge has detained you! Incidentally, keen map-readers will spot that the Landranger and Pathfinder sheets show differences in the route between Aldermaston and Woolhampton. In this case, the line shown on the Landranger sheet actually corresponds with what your feet will find on the ground.

Historical Notes

Woolhampton is said to derive its name from a Saxon warrior. The settlement was mentioned in Domesday as Ollavintone, although by Chaucer's time the contemporary name was in regular usage. In medieval England, Woolhampton was a part of Windsor Forest. The village is in two distinct parts. Upper Woolhampton lies on a southern spur of the Berkshire Downs, high above the A4. It is here that we find St Peter's church, a largely Victorian rebuilding. The Roman Catholic Douai Abbey and College also stand high on the hilltop, where the construction of the Abbey Church only commenced in 1928. This modern creation has a red-brick exterior, with white stone being used for the internal embellishment. Douai was the first Benedictine house in Berkshire since the great abbeys at Abingdon and Reading were abolished by Henry VIII. At the foot of the hills lies the main village, strung out along the Bath Road. This is the Kennet Valley where the river, the Bath Road, the K & A Canal and the main West of England Railway lie cheek by jowl. The history of inland transport could be vividly illustrated from such evidence. The most amusing transport tale hereabouts, however, is why Woolhampton Station is actually named Midgham, the name of a neighbouring village. This dates back to the early days of the GWR when confused passengers were apt to mix up Woolhampton with Wolverhampton, hence the change of name in 1873. The station nameboards still give a quaint touch of the unusual, proclaiming 'Midgham for Douai School'. Where Station Road joins the Bath Road, the observant visitor will quickly spot the Victorian brick structure known to locals as 'the fountain'. This was presented to the village by the late Miss Charlotte Blyth of Woolhampton House, and is the site of an artesian well sunk to provide water to homes along the Bath Road. The shelter around the well was erected during the Diamond Jubilee of Queen Victoria. For members of the public, a drinking fountain was placed inside the construction, whilst four-legged friends could have their thirsts quenched from an external horse trough. To commemorate the erection of the fountain, a plaque reads:

'Righteousness Exalteth a Nation.
Victoria RI Diamond Jubilee 1897.'

The River Kennet Navigation: The river Kennet had been navigable for one mile from its confluence with the Thames in Reading since the 13th century. In 1708, plans were presented to Parliament to canalise the river upstream as far as Newbury, a distance of 18½ miles. As well as utilising the Kennet, the project involved cutting 11½ miles of new canal, together with the construction of 20 locks to overcome a 130 ft rise. The Kennet Navigation Act was approved in 1715, and in 1718 John Hore of Newbury was appointed chief engineer to the project. Not everyone was pleased with the venture, however. Reading merchants had enjoyed monopoly powers in the distribution of goods to the west of their town for many years. They clearly saw some of this privilege heading down to the Newbury burghers. The Navigation posed a threat to their livelihood, so much so that in 1720 the Mayor of Reading led a march of 300 men intent on destroying the works that were underway! Their efforts cannot have come to much, however, for John Hore and his men had completed what amounted to a £45,000 project by 1723. This was a full 71 years before Parliament passed the Kennet & Avon Canal Act to extend the waterway westwards to Bath. Walk 15 explores a section of the Navigation between Woolhampton and Padworth Bridge.

The features along this section of the waterway include Woolhampton Bridge, Aldermaston Lock and Wharf, Aldermaston Lift Bridge, Padworth Lower Wharf and Padworth Lock, a choice selection of canalside architecture. **Woolhampton Bridge** has recently been rebuilt to produce an efficient and functional construction. A 1940 commentary, however, reveals the sad state into which the old swing-bridge had fallen:

'With half the able-bodied males of the village heaving on crow-bars under the direction of the red-faced landlord of the 'Row Barge' and with Cressy going full astern, her bow line fast to a bridge railing post, it took us three hours to open the bridge at Woolhampton.'

When boat traffic on the K & A ceased, a similar swing-bridge at Aldermaston had been 'fixed' in position, posing a real threat to the K & A's eventual restoration. Today, a hydraulic lift-bridge has been introduced in its place, often the cause of impatient queues of traffic on the severed A340! Alongside the lift-bridge is the site of **Aldermaston Wharf**, actually 1½ miles to the north-east of the village. The wharf served as an outlet for local goods, including timber and timber products, malt and flour. Between Aldermaston Lock and the lift-bridge, an arm of the canal branches off to the north. This arm was cut in the 1850s, shortly after the GWR took control of the waterway, and linked the K & A with the neighbouring railway line. As such it formed a useful exchange point for railway and canal traffic. The area around Aldermaston Lock, with its ornately scalloped brickwork, is such a treasure-trove for the industrial archaeologist that a lockside information panel has been erected by the BWB.

Just east of Aldermaston Wharf is **Lower Padworth Wharf**, where the BWB have sited their eastern section canal depot. This was relocated from Newbury in 1967, and sits opposite an old malthouse. This was formerly a branch of Strange's Brewery, although the premises are now used for other light industrial purposes.

If all this talk of industry, industrial archaeology and the ilk leaves you cold, then take some consolation in the fact that the K & A is still a natural paradise in the vicinity. Just before Padworth Lock, I once witnessed an angler jump into the canal when a local ferret took him by surprise. He assured me that a fellow angler had had quite a chunk taken out of his leg by an identical creature just the week before!

Aldermaston has been rendered by one authority as 'the tun of the ealdorman', although quite what that means remains a mystery to me! The village is forever associated with the 'Ban the Bomb' marches that took place each Easter throughout most of the post-war period. Large numbers of pacifists, and many a fledgling MP, would descend upon the Berkshire village, which houses the Atomic Weapons Research Establishment. This is one of those top-secret locations that even the OS is obliged to omit from its maps, and being hidden behind the walls of Aldermaston Court, it is not likely to spoil your enjoyment of what is a fine village. A manor house has existed on the site for many centuries, with both Edward II (1321) and Elizabeth I (1558 and 1601) being just two of its more notable visitors. Alongside the Court grounds, high above the Kennet Valley, sits St Mary the Virgin church. In keeping with the theme of secrecy, it is almost impossible to secure access to the church due to the keeper of the keys retaining his anonymity. Serious writers, however, are all convinced that St Mary's possesses some first-rate medieval wall paintings and a Jacobean seven-sided pulpit. The main street in the village is lined with red-brick and timber buildings, interspersed with the occasional Elizabethan cottage. Facing up the main street is the Hind's Head Inn, whose origins date back to 1650. In the 19th century, the Hind's Head was known as the Congreve Arms, the Congreve family then owning much of the village. Unusually for an inn, the Hind's Head is dominated by a clock tower, topped out with a gilt fox weather-vane. In keeping with many other ancient villages, Aldermaston possesses a traditional candle auction. This is held triennially in December, and the object is to auction the grazing rights associated with Church Acres. A nail is hammered into the candle one inch below the wick, and the rights pass to the highest bidder when the nail falls away from the lighted candle.

Reading and the Thames

Introduction: For eastbound travellers, Reading and Kennet Mouth will be the climax of all the rambles in this book. It is here that the Kennet & Avon Canal joins Old Father Thames. The 85 mile journey from Hanham through to County Lock in Reading has involved over 100 locks as the canal has climbed to its summit at Crofton before descending into the Thames Valley – impressive statistics indeed! The approach to Reading sees fields and meadows being increasingly replaced by urban development – motorways and railways, factories and housing. It must be remembered, however, that canals were not originally cut to provide a leisure resource for walkers or water-borne travellers. Towns like Reading provided the K & A with its very raison d'etre. The landscape will actually be of secondary importance on this occasion, for this is a walk with a goal. Explorers of the K & A Canal will treat Kennet Mouth and the Thames as some sort of pinnacle to be scaled, akin to Yr Wyddfa for hill-walkers in Snowdonia!

Distance: This non-circular walk involves 9 miles of level towpath and river-bank walking. Return by public transport (see below). Maps: OS Landranger Sheet 175 'Reading and Windsor'; Pathfinder Sheet SU 66/76 together with SU 67/77.

Refreshments: Both Theale and Reading at either end of the walk contain many inns and public houses. Perhaps most opportune are the Fisherman's Cottage and the Jolly Angler, alongside Blake's Lock in Reading.

How to get there: Theale lies just off of the M4 motorway at junction 12, midway between Newbury and Reading. There is ample room for parking at the well signposted railway station. (GR 644 709)
NB This is a linear walk from Theale to Reading with the return

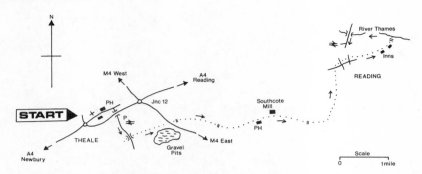

journey being by train. The regular train services can be confirmed by phoning Reading 595911. Alternatively, bus and taxi services operate from outside the station.

The Walk: This linear walk is very straightforward, so much so that the directions could read 'join the K & A at Theale and follow the towpath to Reading'! Perhaps a few more guidelines are in order, however, especially with regard to the various landmarks and features en route.

Leave Theale Station carpark and follow the adjoining road southwards, across the railway line, for just ½ mile to the K & A Canal. Cross the waterway and turn left onto the towpath. The right-of-way keeps to the south bank of the canal for the first mile through to Hissey's Bridge, with the landmarks being Sheffield Lock, Garston Lock, a vast flooded gravel pit and the overbridge carrying the M4 motorway. Garston Lock is the sole surviving turf-sided lock on the waterway, and as such is an undoubted highlight of this walk.

Cross to the north bank of the K & A at Hissey's Bridge, and continue eastwards for another mile to Swan's Roving footbridge. On this section of the waterway, you will leave the river Kennet to follow the Burghfield Cut, an artificial channel constructed to avoid some of the circuitous wanderings of the natural river. Swan's Roving, where the towpath reverts to the south bank of the K & A, lies just to the east of Burghfield Lock. The path keeps to the south bank of the canal for the next couple of miles through to Fobney Lock, with the next series of landmarks being the Cunning Man public house, Southcote Mill and Pumping Station and the artificial Fobney Cut.

At Fobney Lock, return to the north bank of the canal and continue along the towpath for close on 2 miles until you reach the overbridge in the centre of Reading carrying the Inner Distribution Road. This is essentially an urban section of towpath with a landscape to match! You are forced to leave the K & A having passed beneath the Distribution Road, since the next section of towpath no longer exists as a public right-of-way. It was sold off as part of a property deal when the canal was very much in decline!

Cross the K & A by means of the overbridge and follow the pavement alongside the main road for 200 yards to a busy round-about, County Lock on your left-hand side. Continue straight ahead at the roundabout, following the main road that runs alongside Reading's main bus depot. Bus enthusiasts may well spot some veteran models lurking within its confines! Just past the bus depot, turn left into Duke Street which very shortly crosses the K & A.

Rejoin the towpath, now on the south bank of the waterway, and follow the waterway for just over one mile through to Kennet Mouth and the Thames. On this section of the K & A, the jurisdiction over the waterway passes into the hands of the Thames River Authority who actually control Blake Lock. At Kennet Mouth, pass under the railway bridges before crossing the Kennet by means of the Listed Horseshoe Bridge to join the south bank of the Thames. Follow the riverside path westwards for just under a mile to Caversham lock.

Just beyond the lock, leave the river at the road bridge and turn left to head into Reading town centre. Reading General Station lies just 400 yards ahead, and a 10 minute train journey will have you back in Theale. Bus and taxi services also operate from outside the station.

Historical Notes

Theale has enjoyed a long history of human settlement. Excavations in the 19th century during the construction of the GWR unearthed ancient pottery and tool fragments, together with relics of ancient burial sites. Archaeologists were able to conclude that there had been settlement in the area as far back as the early Iron Age (700 BC). The village rose in importance during medieval times, becoming head of a 'Hundred' or administrative district. It has been transport develop-ments, however, that have been the cause of most of Theale's growth. Traditionally, the village lay on the Bath Road and acted as a staging post in the heyday of the horse-drawn carriage. The High Street contained an inordinate number of inns where travellers could partake of 'cake and ale' whilst the horses were refreshed at roadside pumps. 'Little Sodom' was an oft-used phrase amongst devout chapel folk in Theale concerned at the high level of alcohol abuse in ale houses such as the Angel and the Castle! The K & A Canal, the GWR, the A4 trunk road and the M4 motorway have all followed in turn, bringing various degrees of prosperity to the village. Today, the local rail service is vital for residents commuting to Reading and London, whilst the proximity of the M4 has attracted a large number of light industrial premises to the area. Fortunately, the village centre is bypassed by both the A4 and the M4, leaving it with a quiet and tranquil air. Totally dominating the village is a vast early Gothic Revival church, consecrated in 1832 by the Bishop of Salisbury. Holy Trinity was allegedly modelled upon Salisbury Cathedral, although the authenticity of such a claim is somewhat spoiled by a building that possesses towers rather than a vast spire! The experts are all in agreement when, without exception, they note that 'the church is certainly more impressive externally than internally'. Those visitors attracted within her walls are normally drawn to a 15th century stone shrine moved to Theale from Magdalen College, Oxford, by Dr Routh, a one-time College President. Until 1832, Theale was a tithing of nearby Tilehurst, whose Rector from 1810 was Dr Routh. The shrine screens the tomb of his sister, Sophia Sheppard, who donated the funds for the church to be built.

Reading: The town's original prosperity can be traced back to the Benedictine monks who at one time had a virtual monopoly of the town's commerce and trade. The town actually grew up alongside the banks of the Kennet, rather than the Thames, where the monks had control of a portion of the river that included a 'flash lock' or single gate known as 'Brokenburghlok'. Their abbey was one of the largest and richest Benedictine monasteries in England, whose origins and foundations date back to 1121 and Henry I. Subsequent Royal patronage served to enhance the wealth and power of the Abbot to the point where he controlled navigation, milling and fishing rights on the river, as well as being responsible for regulating the trade and markets of the town and electing the Mayor and Warden of the Merchant Guild. What followed is the old story. In 1539, Abbot Faringdon refused to recognise Henry VIII as head of the Church of England, he was subsequently tried for high treason and found guilty, and his punishment was to be hung, drawn and quartered within sight and sound of the abbey. The building was razed, and the stone recycled by local residents for various building projects. The Abbey

Ruins, dominated by the restored Inner Gateway, lie but a short distance from Reading General Station and are worth visiting at the end of the walk before returning to Theale.

Two of the most savoury characters in Reading's history are Messrs Thomas Huntley and George Palmer. The two partners opened a small shop in London Street in 1826 where the manufacture and sale of cakes and biscuits took place. The business – Huntley and Palmer – proved such a success that by 1849 they had moved to a 35 acre site alongside the navigable Kennet. The river was actually used by the company for the unloading of flour and the export of biscuits to London Docks until the Second World War. The company's statistics are truly impressive: the workforce grew from 41 in 1846 to 5,000 by 1900, with up to 400 kinds of cakes and biscuits being manufactured at the site in its heyday. The 'For Sale' signs that recently adorned the premises told their own sad tale, and when you read these notes it may well be the case that the Huntley and Palmer site is nothing more than another riverside development of shops and offices.

So much more could be written of Reading – its coaching traditions, its brewing industry, perhaps even its gaol forever immortalised by Oscar Wilde. His *Ballad of Reading Gaol* was inspired after an enforced two year visit to the grim prison building. The interested reader is referred to an excellent publication – *The Story of Reading* by Daphne Phillips. This book is also published by Countryside Books.

The Kennet & Avon Canal: Between Reading and Theale, most of the route utilises the navigable river Kennet, with just a few short sections of artificial cut. These were designed to avoid the more circuitous wanderings of the river. It is quite an easy exercise to spot these cuts, which are generally more direct and slower moving than the river. Originally this was the Kennet Navigation, opened in 1723 to link Reading and Newbury (see notes in Walk 15). For canal enthusiasts, **Garston Lock** (number 102) will be an undoubted highlight of this walk. Garston is the sole surviving turf-sided lock on the waterway. Locks on the Kennet Navigation were all originally constructed to this design, with timber lining the sides to 2 ft below the lock's lower level, above which turfed sides sloped away at an angle of 45 degrees. Lacking an upper retaining wall, these historical oddities are deemed as unsafe by today's planners and engineers, and have been gradually replaced by functional but less aesthetic modern constructions. Two miles on from Garston is **Southcote Pumping**

Station, now a private residence, which was opened in 1850 to lift water from the Kennet to a reservoir on the Bath Road that supplied the residents of Reading with their water. Its replacement, the Fobney Works, stands alongside Fobney Lock a mile or so to the east. Just beyond the Inner Distribution Road Bridge in the centre of Reading lies lock 106 on the K & A – **County Lock**. This is the last official lock on the waterway, although there remains one further lock before Kennet Mouth. Blake's Lock, although on the Kennet, is overseen by the Thames River Authority, their only lock not on the Thames itself. Between County Lock and Blake's, the K & A passes through the infamous **Brewery Gut**. This narrow, enclosed section of the Kennet was constructed in the 1880s when Simmond's Brewery bought the towpath alongside the river for development, forcing the waterway into a treacherous channel. At the time, it was thought that canals and inland waterways were in permanent decline and could be slowly pensioned off. Today traffic lights are used to ensure that one-way traffic only passes through the narrow 'Gut' whilst walkers are forced away from the canalside onto the neighbouring streets due to lack of a towpath.

At Kennet Mouth, a ferryman was originally employed to take any towing horse across to the far bank of the river if their craft were about to head westwards along the Thames. The first such appointment was back in 1810 where the horses were conveyed at 2d a time. In 1892, the GWR constructed the **Horseshoe Bridge** to replace the ferry, its name being self-explanatory. This construction is, together with Brunel's adjoining railway bridge, a Listed building, and forms a fitting climax to the eastern end of the waterway.

It is impossible to do justice to Reading's canalside environment in a volume of this nature. Interested readers are referred to the K & A Canal Trust's Towpath Guide no. 12 *Reading – Southcote to Kennet Mouth*. Equally, a visit to **Blake's Lock Museum** (whose location should be obvious!) is another source of information. Telephone Reading 575911 for details of opening times.